FASTNESS

TREVOR JOYCE

Fast

MIAMI UNIVERSITY PRESS

ness

A TRANSLATION FROM THE ENGLISH OF

EDMUND SPENSER

Library of Congress Cataloging-in-Publication Data

Names: Spenser, Edmund, 1552?–1599. | Joyce, Trevor, 1947– translator, author.

Title: Fastness : a translation from the English of Edmund Spenser / by Trevor Joyce.

Description: Oxford, Ohio : Miami University Press, 2017.

Identifiers: LCCN 2016051549 | ISBN 9781881163619 (print)

Subjects: LCSH: Spenser, Edmund, 1552?–1599. Mutabilitie Cantos.

Classification: LCC PR2358.A21 2017 | DDC 821/.3—dc23

LC record available at https://lccn.loc.gov/2016051549

Designed by Quemadura

Printed on acid-free, recycled paper

in the United States of America

Miami University Press

356 Bachelor Hall

Oxford, OH 45056

FOR

TOM RAWORTH

PADDY GALVIN

MIKE SMITH

GOOD COMPANIONS

INTRODUCTION

all things hate fixity, and so see
themselves translated

Spenser's poem, *The Faerie Queene*, is generally agreed to be the greatest English non-dramatic poem of its age, but that age was five centuries ago. Even in its time, it was seen as a little strange, composed in an artificially archaic dialect in an obscure high allegorical mode, and though it's one of the longest poems in the English language, Spenser seems never to have finished it, though we have, maybe, a fragment of a completion.

Now, in such different times, can such a freak speak to us? I think it can. Let me try to explain.

*

The basic plot is simple. Jove is the universal overlord in the world of these cantos, an autocrat with a savage temper and a history of violence, including torture. A challenger emerges in the form of Mutability, named for her propensity to stir things up, to disrupt even the most settled states. Her first target is Cynthia, the moon.

Jove moves to slap down this rival with a combination of patronising flattery and menace, but rather than giving in Mutability calls him out on his right to rule.

Her father, Titan, was the elder brother of Jove's father, Saturn. Saturn tricked Titan out of his right to rule, and since then his line has dominated solely by force of arms, she says. Now she challenges his position, and the entire order of things he has established.

Choosing law rather than physical force, Mutability insists on being heard by the highest court, where Nature is the judge. She calls many witnesses to show from experience how those powers which actually make the universe work have always obeyed her rule.

When Jove tries again to put her down, she argues that he and his henchmen, despite their high claims, have risen from low beginnings, and that, in fact, she already rules them though they refuse to acknowledge it, and hide their origins.

The Judge listens carefully, weighs the evidence a while, and delivers her brief verdict. She acknowledges the force of Mutability's case, but then abruptly introduces new evidence herself, from a quarter neither Mutability, nor even Jove, has invoked, and on the strength of that declares Jove the winner.

It's the stuff of Marvel Comics, a story populated with superheroes battling for control of the universe, and it seems ready-made for a sequel in which the feisty heroine returns, this time choosing force rather than law, to overthrow the unjust system which, for a second time, had tried to defraud her of her rights.

If there has been any such sequel, it was played out in the realm of history rather than in Spenser's poem.

*

Spenser was born in London around the year 1552. His family was not wealthy, and he qualified to receive material assistance from the University in Cambridge to allow him to study there. In 1579 he married, and also published *The Shepherds Calendar*, a pastoral sequence in which he himself figured as the shepherd Colin Clout.

In July of 1580, he sailed to Ireland in the service of Lord Grey of Wilton, who, as Queen Elizabeth's Deputy, had assembled an army of about 6,000 soldiers to put down the Desmond Rebellion there. This was only the most recent in a series of such uprisings, in which the extension of English control was complicated by religious and cultural hostilities, by rivalries among "Old English" dynastic families, the descendants of the twelfth-century Norman invaders, and even by aftershocks from the English War of the Roses.

Spenser was Secretary to Lord Grey, and along with Walter Raleigh attended him as his army besieged, and then massacred, a force of about 600 Italian and Spanish soldiers at Smerwick, in County Kerry. These were Catholic troops, supporting Papal ambitions. According to several reports, those soldiers had surrendered their arms on the promise of mercy. It was a group under

Raleigh's command that "entered into the castell & made a great slaughter." Those not immediately put to the sword were later hanged, including women and children camp-followers, while the priests among them first had their bones broken by a blacksmith's hammer.[1]

Great wealth was to be got from these Irish wars, and after Grey had been recalled to England to answer charges of malfeasance in 1582, Spenser remained in Ireland, having acquired both posts and lands to repay his service. By 1589 he had gained his main estate, Kilcolman Castle, in north County Cork, and it was there that most of *The Faerie Queen* was written.

About a year later Spenser traveled to London, to take advantage of the publication there of the first three books of his great work. The volume included a Letter to Raleigh, outlining the intent and structure of the poem, which was to comprise twelve books in all. He won a life pension from the Queen, but may have been irked by failure to pay on time, and he made powerful enemies at court.

In 1594, his first wife having died, he married Elizabeth Boyle, a relation of Richard Boyle, a younger man already on the rise, who went on to become one of the great tycoons of the age, and later Earl of Cork, thanks to his land-grabbing exploits in Ireland.

In 1596 Spenser wrote, in defence of Lord Grey, a prose dialogue, *A View of the Present State of Ireland*, in which he described in some detail the effects of famine in Ireland, and encouraged the pacification of the country by a scorched earth policy, and the eradication of Irish language and culture. Perhaps because of the sensitivity of the subject, the *View* was circulated only in manuscript and not published until 1633, several decades after Spenser's death.

He did publish several other works about this time, however. Most important was a second installment of three books of *The Faerie Queen*. Also notable, though, was *Colin Clouts Come Home Againe*, a partly autobiographical pastoral poem based on Spenser's visit to London five years earlier. He dedicated it to Raleigh, who figures in the poem as the Shepherd of the Ocean, as Spenser himself was disguised as the Colin Clout of the title.

*

It is from this point that Spenser's life reads as a sequel, radically translated, to *The Mutability Cantos*, which he was likely finishing at about this time. The imperial theme was already sounded in his dedication to the 1590 edition of *The Faerie Queene* "To the most mightie and magnificent Empresse Elizabeth, by the grace of god, Queene of England, France and Ireland," and England's foothold in Ireland was maintained, Jove-like, only by force of arms, against both the Old English descendants of the Normans, led amongst others by the Earl of Desmond, and the Gaelic Irish, both with a strong prior claim to rule in Ireland.

During these years, Spenser continued to acquire estates in Cork in the continuing landrush. Along with Raleigh, he participated enthusiastically in the Munster Plantation. As settler colonists, both amassed significant holdings, Raleigh particularly so since, due perhaps to an administrative error in addition to his good connections, he was allocated a conspicuously vast estate.

The estates gained by Spenser, Raleigh, Boyle, and their fellow settlers comprised the lands of those who had joined with the Earl of Desmond in resisting English power in the southern province of Ireland. That is, this was confiscated land redistributed to the English 'planters'.

The system of settler colonisation first tried out by the English in their earlier plantations in Ireland[2] was further perfected at this time both in Munster and in the Lost Colony at Roanoke, and soon extended to their conquests elsewhere in North America and the Caribbean.

The outbreak of hostilities, later known as The Nine Years War, which had started in the northern counties of Ireland in 1594, reached the southern province of Munster, and as the native Irish forces of Hugh O'Neill approached Spenser was forced to abandon Kilcolman in 1598. He fled to Cork city, and some reports claimed an infant son died in the blaze when the castle was burned out.

Spenser went again to London, seeking support, but died there, aged 46, "for lack of bread" as Ben Jonson put it, in 1599.

*

It was only in 1609, a decade after the poet's death, that the six books of *The Faerie Queen* were reissued in a single volume, along with a previously unpublished fragment, titled by the publisher as *Two Cantos of Mutabilitie*. This fragment ended with two stanzas apparently belonging to yet a third canto.

The relationship of these elements to one another, and to the six completed books of *The Faerie Queen*, is the subject of much discussion. The publisher remarked that they, "both for Forme and Matter, appeare to be parcel of some following Booke of *The Faerie Queene*, under the Legend of *Constancie*." Some have argued that, rather than being a fragment, the new cantos make up a coherent whole, and despite superficial similarities, could never have fitted into any extension of *The Faerie Queen*, as we see it both in the completed six books, and in Spenser's letter to Raleigh.

The structure of the first six books centers on a Fairy Court from which knights are sent off on quests, and to which they come back, all having been helped by Prince Arthur at some stage. In his Letter to Raleigh, Spenser writes that the purpose of the poem "is to fashion a gentleman or noble person in vertuous and gentle discipline." The focus, then, is on ethics, how one should bear oneself. He also describes it as "a continued Allegory, or darke conceit," and so, despite his own attempts to clarify what's happening in the poem, most modern readers find it necessary to equip themselves with a heavily annotated edition, explaining the obscure words and making clear who's who, what they're doing, and why they're doing it. If you like beautiful language you'll find some fine passages in *The Faerie Queene*, but without help much may seem tedious, confused, and hopelessly obscure.

Certainly these additional *Mutability Cantos* seem different from what went before, and though originally presented as a fragment of a larger, and now lost, whole, they have a unity, and a power which encourages us to read them on their own, and to see them as the climax of Spenser's achievement as a poet. Though the argument is complex, the basic narrative needs little help to decode beyond a basic acquaintance with Classical mythology. They differ also in that their focus is on what and how things are, on metaphysics and on politics.

It's as if, through its many years of composition, and perhaps as a result of Spenser's experiences as landholder and colonial administrator in England's

Munster colony, *The Faerie Queen* stepped out of itself and became something quite different from what the poet first intended: less sure of itself, less dependent on the English court, but even more ambitious in its reach.

The Mutability Cantos' motif of a settled kingdom disrupted by insurgents citing a prior claim has clear resonances in Elizabethan Ireland. As Spenser himself noted, "the Methode of a Poet historicall is not such, as of an Historiographer," but he had already blurred fact with fiction by writing himself and his friend Raleigh into his poem *Colin Clouts Come Home Again*, and in his Letter to Raleigh, he had identified the figure of Cynthia as representing Elizabeth. It's no wild fantasy to find Spenser's anxiety as settler colonist refracted through the dark glass of his late poetry.

Apart from the way the basic plot of *The Mutability Cantos* resonates with the history of Spenser's last years, its own history and its condition of doubtful ruin can seem to exemplify its themes. It was first published as a fragment of a larger whole which had been lost, a completed twelve-book epic of *The Faerie Queen*. But there is little to suggest that *The Faerie Queen* was in fact ever completed, and it's less than entirely clear how *The Mutability Cantos*, as they stand, could have fitted into such a work. Instead, these two and a bit cantos seem to have a wholeness of their own, with no need of connection to the earlier published books.

The status of the text, between fragment and whole, between medieval literary romance and document of Elizabethan history, is paralleled by Queen Elizabeth's own appearance in the poem, as Cynthia / Diana, wholly within the tale on the one hand, but being criticised for real policies on the other.

*

I said the basic narrative was simple. There is, however, a secondary plot, occupying just under a sixth of the text, but whose essentials are no more difficult to grasp.

When Mutability appeals to Dame Nature's Court, the meeting of that court is set to occur on the summit of Arlo Hill. This is Spenser's name for Galtymore, the tallest mountain in the Galty range, which itself continues the arc of the Ballyhouras, and all of which Spenser names as Old Father Mole. The name

Arlo clearly echoes that of the Glen of Aherlow, which lies just north of the Galtys, west of the Ballyhouras. In short, this is a very specific region of Ireland that Spenser has chosen for his court.

His subplot tells how, in this glen, Faunus, half-man and half-beast, played the Peeping Tom on Diana, chaste goddess of the hunt. He was discovered, and, turned entirely beast, cursed always to run, pursued by his own hounds. Diana, though, unsatisfied still, curses even the glen itself, so that all the happy idylls there were stopped, and it reverted to a natural state, a dangerous haunt of wolves and human miscreants.[3]

Here we have another intersection of Spenser's fictions with the realities which surrounded him. The Glen of Aherlow was in his day truly frequented by wolves, and had been a stronghold of the insurgents during the Desmond Rebellions. For settler agriculturalists like Spenser it really was a threat. This sub-plot suggests that the dangerous wilderness of Aherlow was due to its abandonment by Elizabeth/Diana.

*

There is one final, and very brief, section of the Cantos which I haven't yet discussed: the final two stanzas. We have just had both Mutability, the court plaintiff, and Nature, the Judge, declaim strongly in the first person.[4] Now a completely new voice is introduced, also speaking in the first person, weighing up both Mutability's plea and Nature's judgement. This intervention is as surprising as Nature's *volte face* in which she awards the verdict to Jove, and when, having quoted both earlier speakers, Spenser combines in a profound pun in Hebrew (Sabaoth) the hope of peace and of military force, it reads perhaps most readily as the poet's putting his own faith, as English planter in a hostile land, in the religiously motivated force of Elizabeth's Protestant armies.[5]

*

For the modern reader with a knowledge of this background, Spenser's *Mutability Cantos* resonate strongly not just as poetic fantasy, but also as an intervention in the history of his time that parallels his prose tract, *A View of the Present State of Ireland*.

In terms of the the contest outlined in the Cantos, the *View* itself aligns with Jove's scheme of things: what we have we will hold by any means necessary.[6]

Cromwell, the savagery of whose campaign in Ireland renders him still notorious here, was an admirer of Spenser,[7] but it was not the poetry that interested him but the repressive strategies outlined in the *View*.[8] And I would suggest that it was *The Down Survey of Ireland*, carried out by William Petty so that Cromwell could pay off his troops, and investors from the City of London, that was the primary factor in the translation of Irish land to English property in the seventeenth century. A major effect of this translation was to cut Ireland off from its own history, to make possible the claim that the Irish were barbarians, without culture or a past worth the slightest regard.[9]

Though Jove is awarded the verdict by Nature, the main thrust of the Cantos runs contrary to this. Mutability's insistence on genealogy opens to question the history of how things have come to be as they are, and how the Universe has been divided.[10] In her challenging of the status quo, her daring to speak truth to power, even straight to the heart of Empire, Mutability stands as poetic ancestor to Milton's Satan and William Blake's great figures of rebellion, and her pageant of witnesses bears comparison with Shelley's *The Masque of Anarchy*.

I hope that I have conveyed some sense of why *The Mutability Cantos* are still important, still worth our attention, both as historical document and as poem. I hope that the reader can imagine too why one might want to respond to them, to read them against the grain, suggesting perhaps that Mutability's charge be met with something more substantial than the anodyne insertion of revealed religion at the end, or that the language in which the whole thing is cast favours those in power against those who challenge and resist.

Recall that "the Methode of a Poet historicall is not such, as of an Historiographer." Poetry worth the name isn't limited to the historian's prose. On encountering a big church-bell for the first time, a child may ping the rim of it, fiddle with the tongue, scrape their nails across the irregular surface, and produce a variety of sounds which may well be interesting in themselves, but when the ropes are pulled and the whole instrument is activated, it's a whole different experience.

Prose delivers events, dates, ideas, and opinions clearly and in sequence; the poet creates a whole in which everything resonates at once: the individual sounds of the consonants and vowels and their rhythms as they interrupt each other, the dictionary meanings of the words and the associated meanings they've gathered through ordinary and specialist use, the whole spectrum of registers from high courtly politeness to low growled threats and back again through slang and vulgarities.[11] Poetry is a complex instrument, and a poet like Spenser knows how to play it to the full, and any response needs to take account of all that. The most adequate, fully engaged response, I would argue, is another poem that picks up all the carefully distributed threads of Spenser's utterance and gives them back radically altered in many ways, but recognizably chiming with the original, and adding new meaning.

*

Language is to the fore in Spenser's *Cantos*.[12] Mutability first shows up as physically disrupting Jove's ordered universe, muscling Cynthia out of her throne, and challenging the entire hierarchy of Gods. Once Jove enters the action, however, she ceases to be a physical threat, and instead puts her trust in Law, resorting like Jove to a high rhetoric of power so she may be allowed to make her case. Can it be any real surprise then, that when, in that sudden *volte face*, the case is settled in Jove's favour, Mutability is left without any comeback: "So was the Titaness put down and whist."[13] She is not only quelled, but deprived of speech. Language, here, is destiny.

The Scottish poet, Tom Leonard, has outlined how "mystification of government" goes in train with "the invention of Literature as a mystery," and how "the Keepers of the Mystery are the Keepers of the Right to Dialogue."[14]

Small wonder, then, that in this great founding work of Literature,[15] written by Queen Elizabeth's would-be court poet, the challenger, when she resorts to the Queen's English, ultimately finds herself whist and without possibility of appeal.

The issue of Irish sovereignty was later translated to the field of war, and settled for some centuries by Cromwell's campaign and Petty's Survey. But since that final stasis, on the promise of which Judge Nature rejected Mutability's pleadings, has not yet arrived, I have taken it on myself to reopen the case, and to give fresh audience to the plaintiff. Remembering that democracy is daily dialogue, and true democracy lies in the equality and equal power of all parties to that dialogue,[16] my primary intervention has been to open the language of the proceedings beyond the precincts of the Queen's English, admitting all parties.

Like Spenser, I've made for myself an artificial dialect. I've tried to dilate my own everyday language, including not only traces of Spenser's lexicon, but also slang, both recent and outmoded, alongside the jargons of journalism, advertising, politics, and business. I've reached after vulgarisms and low catchphrases, and seized on every register that seemed to resist authority. With them I've tried to make a better case for Mutability, and to allow her, now, a jury of her peers.

The primary decision was to aim for speed and idiomatic clarity, as against Spenser's artificially distanced register. He chooses to make his rebel, even in the act of rebellion, subject to the language of governance. This is a way, I'd suggest, to put her in her place right from the beginning, before she even leaves it. Take for example the final quibbling judgement, through which judge Nature leaves Mutability "put down and whist"; it invokes the authority of Scripture, but what plausibility it has derives from its play with learned terms of state, with talk of rule and reigns and states. In fact, as Spenser tells us, Nature herself, even in the instant of arriving at her verdict against Mutability, is in movement, switching from fixed silence to cheerful speech, and yet Mutability, completely untrue to previous form, accedes to this fiction of justice done. The language of power creates pre-emptively the truth it pretends to discover, and the tongue of the oppressed, sounding for only the briefest instance, is named "false" and whist.

I have tried almost always to get away from Spenser's poetic effects. There are a few instances where I have deliberately stayed close in technique, or even identical in phrasing. Spenser frequently resorts to punning, which is just the extreme case of wringing the most sense out of the least verbal material. In particular, when Mutability comes to cite the four elements in her defence, he has her use, repeatedly, almost obsessively, the word *still*. In compactly combining two nearly opposed meanings (on the one hand, stasis, and on the other hand continuance), it serves as a simpler analogue to his final dense pun of *Sabaoth*, so I have taken it as essential to what he is doing, and have largely retained it.

I have introduced one slightly ostentatious pun of my own in using the term *spenser* to translate Spenser's dairying *huswife* (48, 1). As a *spenser* or *spencer* was someone whose job it was to dispence provisions in a household, I have taken the liberty of reinserting the poet into his own text at another point than the privileged one he has chosen for himself, framing the entire action from his own privileged perspective. The role of dutiful assassin of vermin strikes me as neatly rhyming with his land-grabbing activities.[17]

Still on the subject of puns, I must acknowledge my recoil from Spenser's climactic Hebrew wordplay. I don't pretend to any knowledge of the language, and, besides, I would want to express a distance from what may be the poet's own personal witness of faith, while yet not failing to observe it. So, I have chosen to honour Spenser's pun in translation by a distinct one of my own, but in English, which I have also elevated, slightly modified, to be my title. I hope to combine the Jovian notion of stasis (as in "a fast dye") with accelerated processes of mutability and ruin (fast=rapid), while also invoking Spenser's fastness at Kilcolman where he wrote the Cantos, and my thoroughgoing transformation of the text in painting it with bright go-faster stripes.

Freed by time from the mystificatory concerns of Spenser's politics, my aim in all has been to purge the narrative of the surface dazzle of mystery, and to produce instead a work which augments and extends Mutability's genealogical pursuit, seeing in Spenser's project the beginnings not just of a dominant tendency in English poetry, but even the beginnings of Britain's imperial enterprise.

*

One final point. The provocation of claiming this as "Translated from the English of Edmund Spenser" is quite deliberate, and for me intrinsic to its meaning. A short genealogical digression of my own may help clarify.

In 1898, as the eldest of his generation, my great-grandfather, Michael Joyce, wrote what he called a Pedigree of his family. The first progenitor that he could name was a Seán Mór Seoighe (Big Jack Joyce), who in the final decades of the seventeenth century took up work as steward of Lord Kerry's estate at Lixnaw in County Kerry.

The best account of life in that lordly household was written by William FitzMaurice, who rose to be Earl of Shelburne, first Marquess of Lansdowne, and, ultimately, Prime Minister of Great Britain in 1782–3, overseeing the end of the American War of Independence. Of his grandfather, the 20th Lord Kerry, he wrote:

> He was a handsome man, and, luckily for me and mine, married a very ugly woman, who brought into his family whatever degree of sense may have appeared in it, or whatever wealth is likely to remain in it, the daughter of Sir William Petty.

Anne Petty, the wife of this Lord Kerry, and the driving intelligence behind the many building works then undertaken, was indeed the daughter of Sir William Petty, Cromwell's Surveyor. It's probable that Jonathan Swift, a close friend of this Lady Kerry,[18] visited her in Lixnaw while on his tour of southwest Ireland in 1723. Six years later, in 1729, Swift published his *A Modest Proposal for Preventing the Children of Poor People From Being a Burden on the Country, and for Making Them Beneficial to the Public*, the style of which is an evident parody of that of William Petty, Anne's father.[19]

Certainly, though her husband was obstinate, narrow-minded and tyrannical, it was her intent to make Lixnaw a centre of culture, as contemporary accounts of the house describe.

> The seat stands agreeably on the River Brick which is here cut into several pleasant canals that adorn its plantations and gardens. The improvements are very extensive, most of the vistoes and avenues terminating by different buildings, seats, and farmhouses. The tide flows up to the gardens, whereby boats of a considerable burden may bring up goods to the bridge near the house ...
>
> The present house consists of a large building with wings on each side. In one of these wings a chapel, the walls of which are painted in fresco by a foreigner, John Souillard, being copies of the celebrated cartoons of Raphael at Hampton Court, particularly, the lame man healed by Peter and John, Elymas

> the Sorcerer, Paul preaching at Athens, &c. The figures are as large as life, and over the door, between festons and other decorations are the heads of Homer, Virgil, Milton and Pope all in clear obscura by the same hand.[20]

All this she achieved in what her grandson termed "an ignorant neighbourhood".

After a couple of generations, a minor succeeded to the title of Lord Kerry, and the Joyce family moved to Limerick, leaving the Lixnaw estate to fall to ruin.[21] Around a century later, in 1780, they settled in Glenosheen, on the north side of the Ballyhoura Hills (Father Mole), almost directly in line between Spenser's Kilcolman Castle and the Arlo Hill of the Cantos (Galtymore).

Michael Joyce's father, Gearóid an Scoláire (Garrett the Scholar) was a farmer and shoemaker, who "could repeat the Poems of the Iliad and Odyssey with but very few mistakes," and the nickname of his grandfather, Roibeard an Gaelgoir (Robert the Irish-Speaker) indicates also a love of learning and facility in the Irish language. There were others too, poets and musicians and scholars.

Among Michael's brothers, two in particular remembered Spenser's connection with the area. Robert Dwyer Joyce is best known as the author of several uncomplicated Irish nationalist ballads.[22] One of many others he wrote, all of them littered with placenames from this area, is *Kilcoleman Castle*, subtitled *The Burning of Kilcoleman*. Behind its sensational pyrotechnics, it strikes me as a confused and conflicted piece of verse, now in awe of Spenser ("The man of endless fame"), now resentful at his offences against Ireland and its poets in the *View* ("the wizard man who cast the ban / On the minstrels bold and free!"), but finally vengeful, with maybe a hint of self-pity:

> Away sped the galloglasses
> And kerns, all still again,
> Through Houra's lonely passes,
> Wild, fierce, and reckless men.
> But such the Saxon made them,
> Poor sons of war and woe;
> So they venged their strife with flame and knife
> On his head long, long ago!

Robert's elder brother, Patrick Weston Joyce, was the first to gather the traditional identifications of Spenser's landscape with the actual features of the Irish landscape around the Ballyhouras, and to publish the necessary corrections, and several important additions, thereby establishing clearly to what an extent *The Faerie Queene* was an Irish poem.[23]

*

Memory, history, genealogy: as I remarked of Mutability's invocation of genealogy, it's a way of reckoning history, of questioning the status quo, of asking how things have come to be as they are, both personally and from a broader perspective. Questions of what shall be allowed to change until it fall to ruin, and what else shall be declared timeless and eternal, and conserved at all costs, are not matters of science or philosophy, but of politics, and it's through history that we learn both to interpret the world, and to change it.

Jovial elision of history refuses to recognize how privilege and deprivation run through established networks, how wealth, power, and culture are passed down in families, and why we are encouraged to speak in certain registers of language and to disdain others. Is it irrelevant to Spenser's fantasy about the Glen of Aherlow, abandoned to forest and predators, that he named his sons Sylvanus, after the Roman God of Forests, and Peregrine? That his grandson, a Catholic, was one of those dispropriated by Cromwell, and that Edmund Burke, the Eighteenth Century political philosopher, who was related to Spenser and named after him, spent much of his childhood with his mother's family in Shaballymore, where Spenser had owned lands, just six miles from Kilcolman Castle?[24]

There are many reasons why I, an Irish poet, don't respond to Spenser in the Irish language, but only in some form of his English. Prominent among them is that he, Cromwell, and Petty all intervened in my genealogy, the history of my becoming, and so it is that I now intervene in his. It is up to each of us to make what we can of the legacies that come down to us, and this poem, this *Fastness*, is what I've made of mine.

I hope that I've succeeded in casting together my personal inquiry along with more public ones, into this bell, this sounding instrument I've constructed, so that they may reverberate together without significant loss, of Spenser's meaning or of mine.

NOTES

1. For a detailed account and consideration of the events at Smerwick, see Vincent P. Carey, "Atrocity and history: Grey, Spenser and the slaughter at Smerwick" in David Edwards, Pádraig Lenihan, Clodagh Tait, eds., *Age of Atrocity* (Dublin: Four Courts Press, 2007) 79–94.

2. There was, for example, a Leix-Offaly Plantation under Queen Mary in the 1550s, and another in the Ards Peninsula in Ulster in the early 1570s.

3. Its loss to the English sense of order allowed other things than wolves and thieves to flourish there. It was while hiding in the Glen of Aherlow that Geoffrey Keating is said to have written *Foras Feasa Ar Éirinn*, his great *History of Ireland*, which was published in 1634. For discussion of Keating's history in relation to the contemporary first publication of Spenser's View, see Richard McCabe, *Spenser's Monstrous Regiment* (Oxford: Oxford UP, 2002) 276.

4. "I aloft should reare / My Trophee" (VII, 56, 4–5), and "I well consider all that ye haue sayd" (VII, 58, 1).

5. Andrew Hadfield, *Spenser, A Life* (Oxford: Oxford UP, 2012) describes the pun as "profound", and suggests a possible reading as "pointing away from earthly matters towards the peaceful rest promised for the faithful after death" (371). He also reminds us that if the Cantos truly were a fragment, this ending would only have been provisional, and most likely superseded by further reframings.

6. Jove's insistence that the present state of things is necessarily how they must remain is, in its wilful obliteration of history, reminiscent of the facile mantra "we are where we are" much favoured by Irish politicians following their destruction of the Irish economy in the years following the 2008 financial crash.

7. *Spenser, A Life* 411.

8. Cromwell's policies clearly echo those advocated by Spenser, which include "brutal war, state-induced famine, dispossession, transplantation, and the elimination of the Gaelic learned and ruling elites." Carey 81.

9. "Read together, Spenser's View of Ireland and The Cantos of Mutabilitie map Ireland as a desert in order to defend its further wasting through systematic depopulation, geographic reinscription, and georgic recolonization." Julia Reinhard Lupton, "Map-

ping Mutability: or, Spenser's Irish plot" in Brendan Bradshaw, Andrew Hadfield, and Willy Maley, eds., *Representing Ireland: Literature and the Origins of Conflict, 1534–1660* (Cambridge: Cambridge UP, 2010).

10. Gordon Teskey, "Mutability, Genealogy, and the Authority of Forms," *Representations* 41(1993): 104–22.

11. By way of condensed example, consider the several complex simultaneous, and in part opposed, meanings compact in the penultimate word of Spenser's text. He puns in Hebrew, the language of the Bible, in a poem very predominantly in English, but which contains many vestiges of classical Latin and Greek, and at least one Irish contaminant ("false Bregog", which plays on the Irish bréag = a lie), and in it he combines notions of rest or peace with armed force.

12. The importance for Spenser of being able to express himself in his own language is pronounced in his expostulation to Gabriel Harvey, "Why a God's name may not we, as else the Greeks, have the kingdom of our own language", which is discussed at length by Richard Helgerson in his *Forms of Nationhood: The Elizabethan Writing of England* (Chicago: University of Chicago Press, 1994).

13. Canto VII, 59, line 6.

14. Tom Leonard, introduction, *Radical Renfrew: Poetry from the French Revolution to World War I* (Edinburgh: Polygon, 1990) xxi.

15. Angus Fletcher says that the Mutabilitie Cantos "belong with The Faerie Queene, which is the founding text or poem for the full-blown English Romantic tradition, and hence for Romanticism itself." See *A New Theory for American Poetry: Democracy, the Environment, and the Future of Imagination* (Cambridge: Harvard UP, 2004) 299.

16. Leonard, quoting Tom Paine.

17. How Spenser's staging of this cosmic drama echoes his own more immediately personal squabbles as grasping landholder is outlined in P. Coughlan, "The Local Context of Mutabilitie's Plea," *Irish University Review* 26:1 (1996): 320–41.

18. In *A Journal to Stella*, he pre-empted her grandson as arbiter of beauty, describing his friend as "most egregiously ugly; but perfectly well bred".

19. I first began looking at these connections in the context of family history over thirty years ago. Some of them are briefly touched on, from a literary point of view, in P. Coughlan, "Cheap and common animals': the English anatomy of Ireland in the seventeenth century" in Thomas Healy and Jonathan Sawday, eds., *Literature and the English Civil War* (Cambridge: Cambridge UP, 2010).

20. William Smith, "The Ancient and Present State of the County of Kerry," 1756.

21. During his Tour of Ireland in 1776, Arther Young noted "October 3rd, left Ardfert, accompanying Lord Crosby to Listowel. Called in the way to view Lixnaw, the an-

cient seat of the Earls of Kerry, but deserted for ten years past, and now presents so melancholy a scene of desolation, that it shocked me to see it. Every thing around lies in ruin, and the house itself is going fast off by thieving depredations of the neighbourhood."

22. Of these, "The Boys of Wexford" and "The Wind That Shakes the Barley" are still occasionally heard.

23. P.W. Joyce published many studies of Irish history, place names, and Hiberno-English, as well as translations of Irish legends and folktales. His account of early Irish landholding practices was used by the Irish revolutionary, James Connolly, while his volume of Old Celtic Romances, passed to Tennyson by Alfred Perceval Graves, father of Robert Graves, provided the basis for *The Voyage of Maeldune*.

24. For the importance of this area as a stronghold of Catholic resistance against the Penal Laws, see L. M. Cullen, "The Blackwater Catholics and County Cork Society and Politics in the Eighteenth Century" in Patrick O'Flanagan and C. G. Buttimer, *Cork History and Society* (Dublin: Geography Publications, 1993) 535–84.

FASTNESS

CANTO VI. 1—3

What man that sees the ever-whirling Wheel
Of Change, the which all mortal things doth sway,
But that thereby doth find, and plainly feel,
How *MUTABILITY* in them doth play
Her cruel Sports, to many Mens decay?
Which that to all may better yet appear,
I will rehearse that whylom I heard say,
How she at first her self began to rear,
'Gainst all the Gods, and th'Empire sought from them to bear.

But first, here falleth fittest to unfold
Her antique Race and Linage ancient,
As I have found it register'd of old,
In *Fairy* Land mongst Records permanent:
She was, to weet, a Daughter by descent
Of those old *Titans*, that did whylome strive
With *Saturn's* Son for Heaven's Regiment.
Whom, though high *Jove* of Kingdom did deprive,
Yet many of their Stem long after did survive.

And many of them, afterwards obtain'd
Great Power of *Jove*, and high Authority;
As *Hecate*, in whose Almighty Hand
He plac'd all Rule and Principality,
To be by her disposed diversly,
To Gods, and Men, as she them list divide:
And drad *Bellona*, that doth sound on high
Wars and Alarums unto Nations wide,
That makes both Heaven and Earth to tremble at her Pride.

1 — 3

How fast things shift and spin
out of control, how fast hordes die;
watch that a while, then tell me
you don't see a force at play in it
greater than us. But not just us.
I've heard how this Mutability one time
rose against all the Gods at once,
to disempire them. So let me tell you.

But first, check out her pedigree,
punctiliously transcribed
from the relevant records
in the permanent archive:
she issued from that race
of Titans who once challenged
Saturn's son, King Jove, for rule
in heaven, then survived defeat.

Some of them did well from this.
To Hecate, for instance, Jove gave
all power to rule, to divvy
as she chose to gods and men.
Bellona got to blazon wars
and scares of wars among all nations
generally, so now both heaven and earth
funk out when she shows proud.

CANTO VI. 4—6

So likewise did this *Titaness* aspire,
Rule and Dominion to her self to gain;
That as a Goddess, Men might her admire,
And heavenly Honours yield, as to them twain.
At first, on Earth she sought it to obtain;
Where she such Proof and sad Examples shew'd
Of her great Power, to many one's great pain,
That not Men only (whom she soon subdu'd)
But eke all other Creatures, her bad doings ru'd.

For, she the face of earthly Things so chang'd,
That all which Nature had establisht first
In good Estate, and in meet Order rang'd,
She did pervert, and all their Statutes burst:
And all the World's fair Frame (which none yet durst
Of Gods or Men to alter or misguide)
She alter'd quite, and made them all accurst
That God had blest; and did at first provide
In that still happy State for ever to abide.

Ne she the laws of Nature only brake,
But eke of Justice, and of Policy;
And Wrong of Right, and Bad of Good did make,
And Death for Life exchanged foolishly:
Since which, all living Wights have learn'd to die,
And all this World is woxen daily worse.
O piteous Work of *MUTABILITY*!
By which, we all are subject to that Curse,
And Death instead of Life have sucked from our Nurse.

4–6

Likewise, this Titanic chit, this
Mutability, ambitioned power
for herself, so men might pay her due
respect, as to that aforementioned pair.
First, she went after it on earth,
and showed such strength to hurt,
that not just men, whom she soon
whipped, but all beasts shrank from her.

She altered the whole set-up.
Everything laid out in proper order,
she delinquently deranged. The frame
of things, which looked too good for gods
or men to fuck with, she switched
utterly, and then what God had blessed,
made cursed, and put an end to all
such happy ever afters.

Broke nature's laws, and justice too,
and policy; made right of wrong,
made good of bad, switched life
for death, so now all we who live
have learned to die, as the world
wanes. Nice work there, Mutability,
to curse us all so we choke and puke up
stale death as our first milk!

CANTO VI. 7—9

And now, when all the EARTH she thus had brought
To her Behest, and thralled to her Might,
She 'gan to cast in her ambitious Thought,
T'attempt th' Empire of the Heaven's hight,
And *Jove* himself to shoulder from his Right.
And first, she past the Region of the Air,
And of the Fire, whose Substance thin and slight,
Made no resistance, ne could her contrair,
But ready passage to her pleasure did prepair.

Thence, to the Circle of the Moon she clamb,
Where *Cynthia* reigns in everlasting Glory,
To whose bright shining Palace straight she came,
All fairly deckt with Heaven's goodly story:
Whose silver Gates (by which there sate an hoary
Old aged Sire, with Hower-glass in hand,
Hight *Time*) she entred, were he liefe or sorry:
Ne staid till she the highest Stage had scan'd,
Where *Cynthia* did sit, that never still did stand.

Her sitting on an Ivory Throne she found,
Drawn of two Steeds, th'one black, the other white,
Environ'd with ten thousand Stars around,
That duly her attended Day and Night;
And by her side, there ran her Page, that hight
Vesper, whom we the Evening-Star intend:
That with his Torch, still twinkling like Twylight,
Her lighten'd all the way where she should wend,
And Joy to weary wandring Travellers did lend

7–9

And then, when she had strong
-armed Earth to be her gimp, she hiked
her notions to celestial turf,
plotting a spectacular ouster
for high Jove himself. So, on
she soared through zones
of air and fire, which made no
obstacle, but gave way to her whim.

She scaled the falling light, up to
that orbit where the moon
has her bright palace, saw there
a veteran counting off days
in sand, but she strode willy
nilly by, and further, further up, right
to the summit where Cynthia sat
that just couldn't stand still.

Her throne was ivory, pulled
by a team of two, one black one
white, and then her escort, some
ten thousand stars by night
and day, with tame Vesper trotting
alongside, the evening star, his dim
torch lighting up her path, cheering
all nightrovers home.

CANTO VI 10—12

Tho when the hardy *Titaness* beheld
The goodly Building of her Palace bright,
Made of the Heaven's Substance, and up-held
With thousand Crystal Pillors of huge hight,
She 'gan to burn in her ambitious Spright,
And t'envy her that in such Glory reign'd.
Eftsoones she cast by Force and tortious Might,
Her to displace; and to her self t' have gain'd
The Kingdom of the Night, and Waters by her wain'd.

Boldly she bid the Goddess down descend,
And let her self into that Ivory Throne;
For, she her self more worthy thereof wend,
And better able it to guide alone:
Whether to Men, whose Fall she did bemoan,
Or unto Gods, whose State she did malign,
Or to th'infernal Powers, her need give Loan
Of her fair Light, and Bounty most benign,
Her self of all that Rule she deemed most condign.

But she that had to her that Sovereign Seat
By highest *Jove* assign'd, therein to bear
Nights burning Lamp, regarded not her Threat,
Ne yielded ought for Favour or for Fear;
But with stern Countenance and disdainful Chear,
Bending her horned Brows, did put her back:
And boldly blaming her for coming there,
Bade her attonce from Heaven's Coast to pack,
Or at her peril bide the wrathful Thunder's wrack.

10–12

No sooner had our hardy Titaness
scoped this flash Palace, its sharp courses cut
out of the very stuff of skies, set
on a crystal colonnade, than she wanted
it, and oh, so very very bad! So envy
and ambition raged in her, till she dethroned
the proper queen of night, and arrogated
to herself the darkness and the tides.

Stand up, you Goddess, and step down!
she said, promoting herself to the top
seat she was so suited to; as, when it came
to ruined humanity, whose fall she grieved,
or to that supreme state of Deities
she inveighed against, or even to the powers
of very Hell, it was herself she saw best
qualified for doling light and sweetness out.

The incumbent, though, installed
by high king Jove himself, to illuminate
the night, thought otherwise,
and loftily repelled her, castigating
her damned cheek the while for even
coming there, and with dire threats
of thunderbolts commanded her
get packing out of heaven and back down.

CANTO VI. 13—15

Yet nathemore the *Giantess* forbare:
But boldly pressing-on, raught forth her hand
To pluck her down perforce from off her Chair;
And there-with lifting up her golden Wand,
Threatned to strike her if she did withstand.
Where-at the Stars, which round about her blaz'd,
And eke the Moon's bright Wagon, still did stand,
All being with so bold Attempt amaz'd,
And on her uncouth Habit and stern Look still gaz'd.

Mean-while, the lower World, which nothing knew
Of all that chaunced here, was darkned quite;
And eke the Heavens, and all the heavenly Crew
Of happy Wights, now unpurvaid of Light,
Were much afraid, and wondred at that sight;
Fearing least *Chaos* broken had his Chain,
And brought again on them eternal Night:
But chiefly *Mercury*, that next doth reign,
Ran forth in haste, unto the King of Gods to 'plain.

All ran together with a great Out-cry,
To *Jove's* fair Palace, fixt in Heavens hight;
And beating at his Gates full earnestly,
'Gan call to him aloud with all their Might,
To know what meant that suddain lack of Light.
The Father of the Gods when this he heard,
Was troubled much at their so strange affright,
Doubting lest *Typhon* were again uprear'd,
Or other his old Foes, that once him sorely fear'd.

13–15

Back down? Our Giantess back down?
No chance! Instead, she pressed ahead,
stretching to unseat her rival with a violent
sideswipe from her golden cosh; and all
the stars were deeply shocked.
Even the moon itself, Cynthia's
blazing vehicle, stalled to eyeball
this rude outrageous outsider.

Concerning this, the lower world was wholly
in the dark, and the heavens little better,
as that carefree crew grew all
at once acquainted with the feel of fear,
figuring bound Chaos suddenly
was on the loose again, with endless night
in tow. So then, next neighbor Mercury, exited
his house in haste, to tip off the King.

Soon the whole bunch of them caught up,
bawling their loudest, congregating right
in front of Jove's well-situated Palace,
demanding to know why the whole
lighting system had simultaneously
gone down. Straight off the Father of the Gods
guessed Typhon or some other of his large
Titanic family had broken jail and free.

CANTO VI. 16—18

Eftsoons the son of *Maia* forth he sent
Down to the Circle of the Moon, to know
The cause of this so strange Astonishment,
And why she did her wonted Course forslow;
And if that any were on Earth below
That did with Charms or Magick her molest,
Him to attach, and down to Hell to throw:
But, if from Heaven it were, then to arrest
The Author, and him bring before his presence prest.

The wing'd-foot God, so fast his Plumes did beat,
That soon he came where-as the *Titaness*
Was striving with fair *Cynthia* for her Seat:
At whose strange sight, and haughty Hardiness,
He wondred much, and feared her no less.
Yet laying Fear aside to do his charge,
At last, he bade her (with bold stedfastness)
Cease to molest the Moon to walk at large,
Or come before high *Jove*, her doings to discharge.

And there-with-all, he on her shoulder laid
His snaky-wreathed Mace, whose awful Power
Doth make both Gods and hellish Fiends affraid:
Where-at the *Titaness* did sternly lour,
And stoutly answer'd, that in evil Hour
He from his *Jove* such Message to her brought,
To bid her leave fair *Cynthia's* silver Bower;
Sith she his *Jove* and him esteemed nought,
No more than *Cynthia's* self; but all their Kingdoms sought.

16–18

He field-promoted Mercury to hit
-man, dispatched him to the orbit
of the Moon, to find the problem,
and to fix it quick: if it was some
terrestrial harrassing her, then terminate,
cast him to hell, no questions asked;
if some celestial, arrest and arraign
him here to answer charge.

Wing-foot he went, so fast his feathers
beating the imaginary air, that soon
he happened where our hardy Titaness
was wrestling with fair Cynthia for her seat;
at that fantastic sight, he gulped, yet dared
to speak: *You must stop bothering*
the moon, or else come with me,
instanter, ma'am, to answer to high Jove.

He slapped her straining shoulder then
with his Caduceus, a mace decked
out with snakes that, quite obscurely, struck
fear into both Gods and Fiends alike. What did
our Titaness do then? She snarled, and detailed
the such deep contempt she had for him, and his
King Jove, and Cynthia, and all she wanted
out of them was all they had, their sovereignty.

CANTO VI. 19—21

The Heaven's Herald staid not to reply,
  But past away, his doings to relate
  Unto his Lord; who now in th'highest Sky,
  Was placed in his principal Estate,
  With all the Gods about him congregate:
  To whom when *Hermes* had his Message told,
  It did them all exceedingly amate,
  Save *Jove*; who, changing nought his Count'nance bold,
Did unto them at length these Speeches wise unfold.

Harken to me awhile, ye heavenly Powers;
  Ye may remember since th'Earth's cursed Seed
  Sought to assail the Heaven's eternal Towers,
  And to us all exceeding Fear did breed:
  But how we then defeated all their Deed,
  Ye all do know, and them destroyed quite;
  Yet not so quite, but that there did succeed
  An Off-spring of their Blood, which did alite
Upon the fruitful Earth, which doth us yet despite.

Of that bad Seed is this bold Woman bred,
  That now with bold Presumption doth aspire
  To thrust faire *Phoebe* from her silver Bed,
  And eke our selves from Heaven's high Empire,
  If that her Might were match to her Desire:
  Wherefore, it now behoves vs to advise
  What way is best to drive her to retire;
  Whether by open Force, or Counsel wise,
Areed ye Sons of God, as best ye can devise.

19–21

Zip, replied the Heaven's Herald, not
so much as a word, but off with him
to clue in his boss, who to H.Q.
had summoned up the general staff
of Gods; and who, when his courier had
astonished them with his extreme
dispatch, unhesitatingly
showed he was their leader, so:

Listen here to me, Celestials;
remember how those Giants,
the cursed seed of Earth, assaulted
our eternal towers, and made us shake;
remember too, we bested and damned
near destroyed them, yet let a remnant
of their brood survive to ramp below,
that still regards us with extreme contempt.

She's one of them, this uppity
trull who plans to toss the moon
out of her silver bed, and even
to evict our selves from this
our lofty empire, if she could
just manage what she would; so, think!
ye Godlets, think! what's best to beat
her back: chicanery, or naked force?

CANTO VI. 22—24

So having said, he ceast; and with his Brow
 (His black Eye-Brow, whose doomful dreaded Beck
 Is wont to wield the World unto his Vow,
 And even the highest Powers of Heaven to check)
 Made sign to them in their degrees to speak:
 Who straight 'gan cast their Counsel grave and wise.
 Mean-while, th'Earth's Daughter, tho she nought did reck
 Of *Hermes'* Message; yet 'gan now advise,
What Course were best to take in this her bold Emprize.

Eftsoons she thus resolv'd; that whilst the Gods
 (After return of *Hermes'* Embassy)
 Were troubled, and amongst themselves at odds,
 Before they could new Counsels re-ally,
 To set upon them in that extasy;
 And take what Fortune, Time and Place would lend:
 So, forth she rose, and through the purest Sky
 To *Jove's* high Palace straight cast to ascend,
To prosecute her Plot: Good On-set boads good End.

She there arriving, boldly in did pass;
 Where all the Gods she found in Counsel close,
 All quite unarm'd, as then their manner was.
 At sight of her they suddain all arose,
 In great amaze, ne wist what way to chose.
 But *Jove*, all fearless, forc't them to aby;
 And in his sovereign Throne, 'gan straight dispose
 Himself more full of Grace and Majesty,
That mote enchear his Friends, & Foes mote terrify.

22–24

He said his piece, then stopped,
giving the assembled Gods the eye,
as if to say, *Speak up! But mind*
your place. Meanwhile, in Moonland,
that hothead daughter of a lawless
race continued to play merry hell
with hierarchies, considering her best
options to achieve her ends.

Aha! She'd hit them right away,
while they were still in shock,
before they could concoct
a counter-scheme; then
she'd seize what chance, time,
place, would offer her; so up then
and off to Jove's high citadel she soared:
a quick start's half the battle.

She sprang to that out-corner of the sky
where the Gods were hatching plans,
and took them all aback; the hubbub
of amazed Divinities caught short
was deafening, but brave King Jove
put order on the lily-livered lot of them,
speechifying from his magisterial
throne, all sober grace and majesty.

CANTO VI. 25—27

That, when the haughty *Titaness* beheld,
All were she fraught with Pride and Impudence,
Yet with the sight thereof was almost quell'd;
And inly quaking, seem'd as reft of Sense,
And voyd of Speech in that drad Audience;
Until that *Jove* himself, her self bespake:
Speak thou frail Woman, speak with confidence,
Whence art thou, and what dost thou here now make?
What idle Errand hast, Earth's Mansion to forsake?

She, half confused with his great Command,
Yet gathering Spirit of her Nature's Pride,
Him boldly answer'd thus to his Demand:
I am a Daughter, by the Mother's side,
Of her that is Grand-mother magnify'd
Of all the Gods, great *Earth*, great *Chaos'* Child:
But by the Father's (be it not envy'd)
I greater am in Blood (whereon I build)
Then all the Gods, though wrongfully from Heaven exil'd.

For, *Titan* (as ye all acknowledg must)
Was *Saturn's* elder brother by Birth-right;
Both, Sons of *Uranus:* but by unjust
And guileful Means, through *Corybante's* Slight,
The younger thrust the elder from his Right:
Since which, thou *Jove*, injuriously hast held
The Heavens rule from *Titan's* Sons by Might;
And them to hellish Dungeons down hast feld:
Witness ye Heavens the truth of all that I have teld.

25–27

Now, when our Heroine saw this,
proud and headstrong though she was,
they also could see how nervous
she grew suddenly, and speechless
too, until King Jove himself addressed her:
Speak up, frail female, speak
with confidence in this fair court of ours,
tell us what idle errand brings you here.

Half-intimidated by such authority,
she nonetheless had spirit enough
to answer back, and cap his clout
with her own worth: *I'll have you know*
my dam was Earth, offspring of Chaos,
and grand-mother to all you Gods; but
on my father's side, I'm higher born
than any God, though exiled from this home.

There's none of you can argue but
that Titan was Saturn's elder sib, both
having the same father, Uranus,
and well you know the trickery
through which he lost his birthright,
and how, since then, you, Jove, have
scammed the sons of Titan of their right
to rule, and shackled them instead.

CANTO VI. 28—30

Whil'st she thus spake, the Gods that gave good ear
  To her bold Words, and marked well her Grace,
  Being of Stature tall as any there
  Of all the Gods, and beautiful of Face,
  As any of the Goddesses in place,
  Stood all astonied, like a sort of Steers;
  Mongst whom, some Beast of strange and foreign Race,
  Unwares is chaunc'd, far straying from his Peers:
So did their ghastly Gaze bewray their hidden Fears.

Till having paus'd awhile, *Jove* thus bespake;
  Will never mortal Thoughts cease to aspire,
  In this bold sort, to Heaven claim to make,
  And touch celestial Seats with earthly Mire?
  I would have thought, that bold *Procrustes'* Hire,
  Or *Typhon's* Fall, or proud *Ixion's* Pain,
  Or great *Prometheus*, tasting of our Ire,
  Would have suffic'd, the rest for to restrain;
And warn'd all Men by their Example to refrain:

But now, this Off-scum of that cursed Fry,
  Dare to renew the like bold Enterprize,
  And challenge th'Heritage of this our Sky;
  Whom what should hinder, but that we likewise
  Should handle as the rest of her Allies,
  And thunder-drive to Hell? With that, he shook
  His Nectar-dewed Locks, with which the Skies
  And all the World beneath for terror quook,
And eft his burning Levin-brond in hand he took.

28–30

Those Gods that troubled to attend to her
assertions, and saw how well she held
herself, being just as tall as any there,
with quite as good a figure too as any
glamorous Goddess, stood by astonished,
the way a herd of castrate oxen might
should some lone unfamiliar beast intrude.
And as they stared at her, she sensed their fear.

Jove paused, for maximum effect,
then: *Mortals! will you never learn?*
Your place is not to barge this
vulgar way to bliss, defiling all you touch.
We had Procrustes fitted to his awkward
bed; insurgent Typhon damned to hell; Ixion
lords it on his agonizing wheel; Prometheus,
you know; what more example do you need?

But now, this jism of that foul breed
comes at it again, dares challenge
our prime pedigree, our aristocracy of sky;
and what can discontinue this, unless we zap
her as we did her kind, harrying to hell
with thunderbolts? His head shook with the ictus
of this speech, and the whole world
flinched back from his blazing arms.

CANTO VI. 31—33

But, when he looked on her lovely Face,
 In which, faire Beams of Beauty did appear,
 That could the greatest Wrath soon turn to Grace
 (Such sway doth Beauty even in Heaven bear)
 He staid his Hand: and having chang'd his Chear,
 He thus again in milder wise began;
 But ah! if Gods should strive with Flesh yfere,
 Then shortly should the Progeny of Man
Be rooted out, if *Jove* should do still what he can.

But thee fair *Titan's* Child, I rather ween,
 Through some vain Error or Enducement light,
 To see that mortal Eyes have never seen;
 Or through Ensample of thy Sister's Might,
 Bellona; whose great Glory thou dost spight,
 Since thou hast seen her dreadful Power below,
 Mongst wretched Men (dismay'd with her affright)
 To bandy Crowns, and Kingdoms to bestow:
And sure thy Worth, no less than hers doth seem to show.

But wote thou this, thou hardy *Titaness*,
 That not the Worth of any living Wight
 May challenge ought in Heaven's Interest;
 Much less the Title of old *Titan's* Right:
 For, we by Conquest of our sovereign Might,
 And by eternal Doom of Fate's Decree,
 Have won the Empire of the Heavens bright;
 Which to ourselves we hold, and to whom we
Shall worthy deem Partakers of our Bliss to be.

31–33

But, when he saw her lovely face,
which could placate the greatest rage
(doesn't beauty do that everywhere?),
he held back, and seemed to soften;
his tone when he resumed was kinder
too: *But ah! When Gods contend
with mortals who wins out? When Jove
strikes how long can flesh withstand?*

*But I suspect there's been some trivial
tomfoolery at work to make you long
for spectacle, you Titan child; or just
maybe you're influenced by your big sis
Bellona; you know the grief she's
caused, precipitating here a fearful
crash, there games of chance for crowns;
yes, you're your sister's sib!*

*But be under no illusions, you fool-
hardy Titaness, that any animate entity
can challenge slightest tittle of our Heavenly
portfolio, least with some yarn of what
once Titan held; through war we conquered,
and we seized, as manifest by destiny,
the Empire of the Heavens; so we now
with our associates hold them for keeps.*

CANTO VI. 34—36

Then cease thy idle Claim thou foolish Girl,
And seek by Grace and Goodness to obtain
That place from which by Folly *Titan* fell;
There-to thou may'st perhaps, if so thou fain
Have *Jove* thy Gracious Lord and Sovereign.
So, having said, she thus to him reply'd;
Cease *Saturn's* Son, to seek by Proffers vain
Of idle Hopes t'allure me to thy side,
For to betray my Right, before I have it try'd.

But thee, O *Jove*, no equal Judg I deem
Of my Desert, or of my dueful Right;
That in thine own behalf may'st partial seem:
But to the highest Him, that is behight
Father of Gods and Men by equal Might;
To weet, the God of Nature, I appeal.
There-at *Jove* wexed wroth, and in his Spright
Did inly grudge, yet did it well conceal;
And bade Dan *Phoebus* Scribe her Appellation seal.

Eftsoons the time and place appointed were,
Where all, both heavenly Powers, and earthly Wights,
Before great Nature's Presence should appear,
For trial of their Titles and best Rights:
That was, to weet, upon the highest hights
Of *Arlo-hill* (Who knows not *Arlo-hill?*)
That is the highest Head (in all Mens sight)
Of my old Father *Mole*, whom Shepheards Quill
Renowned hath with Hymns fit for a rural Skill.

34–36

So quit, you foolish girl, cease
and desist to waste court time; try grace
and goodness to regain what folly lost;
that way, Jove might just favour
to accept you, subject. Then she turned on him:
Don't try, you Saturn's son, to wheedle
me with empty breath, or trick me to betray
those rights I've just now started to enjoy.

I judge you, Jove, an interested party,
hence, no fit adjudicator of my rights;
I rather choose to take my pleadings
to the Supreme Court, and hereby appeal
to Highest Him, Master equally of both Gods
and Men, to wit, the God of Nature. Jove
raged but bit his lip; necessary
papers were signed, sealed and sent.

Time and place were set for strict
assembly of the high Powers of Heaven,
alongside merest men; there, great Nature
would preside, to put to test all rights
and titles. Place: topmost summit of Arlo
massif (You don't know Arlo? You've
not lived!), that crowns the vast mountain
range of Mole, some swain once wrote of.

CANTO VI. 37

And, were it not ill fitting for this File,
To sing of Hills and Woods, mongst Wars and Knights,
I would abate the Sternness of my Stile,
Mongst these stern Stounds to mingle soft Delights;
And tell how *Arlo* through *Diana's* Spights
(Being of old the best and fairest Hill
That was in all this Holy-Islands hights)
Was made the most unpleasant, and most ill.
Mean while, O *Clio*, lend *Calliope* thy Quill.

37

This file is not fit to set simple lyrics in,
of hills, and woods, as background
to the business of war; only hard words will do,
no folderols; only for that I'd tell how Arlo,
which always had the richest uplands in that
entire island, turned, through Diana's spite,
to be most treacherous. Yet now I switch
both theme and tone, to tell of:

CANTO VI. 38—40

Whylome, when *IRELAND* flourished in Fame
Of Wealth and Goodness, far above the rest
Of all that bear the *British* Islands Name,
The Gods then us'd (for Pleasure and for Rest)
Oft to resort there-to, when seem'd them best:
But none of all there-in more pleasure found,
Then *Cynthia*; that is sovereign Queen profest
Of Woods and Forests, which therein abound,
Sprinkled with wholsom Waters, more than most on ground.

But mongst them all, as fittest for her Game,
Either for Chase of Beasts with Hound or Bow,
Or for to shroud in Shade from *Phoebus'* flame,
Or bathe in Fountains that do freshly flow,
Or from high Hills, or from the Dales below,
She chose this *Arlo*; where she did resort
With all her Nymphs enranged on a row,
With whom the woody Gods did oft consort:
For, with the Nymphs, the Satyrs love to play and sport.

Amongst the which, there was a Nymph that hight
Molanna; Daughter of old Father *Mole*,
And Sister unto *Mulla*, fair and bright:
Unto whose Bed false *Bregog* whylome stole,
That Shepheard *Colin* dearly did condole,
And made her luckless Loves well known to be.
But this *Molanna*, were she not so shole,
Were no less fair and beautiful than she:
Yet as she is, a fairer Flood may no Man see.

38–40

Ireland once so fortunate,
the Gods for pleasure,
made of it their first resort,
perfect for R&R, and none
of them was happier there
than Cynthia, aka
Diana of the forests,
recognized queen ruler
of the streams that thread
its superabundant woods.

Her best haunt, to hunt,
whether with hound or bow,
and take afterwards a little
shade, or bathe in fountains
spilled, either from heights,
or through the valley floor,
was Arlo, and her Nymphs
attracted there a throng
of Gods and satyrs, all
intent on their game too.

There was a Nymph
named Molanna, daughter
of the Mole massif, and sib
to lovely Mulla, who once was
fooled by the duplicitous
Bregoge (as Shepherd
Colin blabbed), well she,
though shallow, was
just as lovely
as her sister stream.

CANTO VI. 41—43

For, first, she springs out of two marble Rocks,
  On which, a Grove of Oaks high mounted grows,
  That as a Girlond seems to deck the Locks
  Of some fair Bride, brought forth with pompous Shows
  Out of her Bower, that many Flowers strows:
  So, through the flowry Dales she tumbling down,
  Through many Woods, and shady Coverts flows
  (That on each side her silver Channel crown)
Till to the Plain she come, whose Valleys she doth drown.

In her sweet Streams, *Diana* used oft
  (After her sweaty Chace and toilsome Play)
  To bathe her self; and after, on the soft
  And downy Grass, her dainty Limbs to lay
  In covert shade, where none behold her may:
  For, much she hated sight of living Eye.
  Foolish God *Faunus*, though full many a day
  He saw her clad, yet longed foolishly
To see her naked mongst her Nymphs in privity.

No way he found to compass his Desire,
  But to corrupt *Molanna*, this her Maid,
  Her to discover for some secret Hire:
  So, her with flattering Words he first assay'd;
  And after, pleasing Gifts for her purvay'd,
  Queen-Apples, and red Cherries from the Tree,
  With which he her allured and betray'd,
  To tell what time he might her Lady see
When she her self did bathe, that he might secret be.

41–43

She first springs
from two marble
rocks, within a grove
of oaks, just as a bride,
with flowers in her hair,
steps from her tent,
then she descends through
glades and spinneys till
at lowest level she arrives,
and floods the plain.

In these sweet waters
Diana loved, sweaty
and exhausted from a day
at hunt, to bathe herself,
and linger, private, on the grass,
as she abominated
to be spied by any eye.
But one foolish Faun,
lusted to sight her
Naked with her Nymphs.

To achieve this end,
Faunus corrupted Molanna,
the stream, with flattery
first, then gifts, red
cherries and choice apples,
freshly picked, and so
proceeded to demand: the low
-down as to where and when
her Lady bathed, so he
could play Peeping Tom.

CANTO VI. 44—46

There-to he promis'd, if she would him pleasure
With this small Boon, to quit her with a better;
To weet, that whereas she had out of measure
Long lov'd the *Fanchin*, who by nought did set her,
That he would undertake, for this to get her
To be his Love, and of him liked well:
Besides all which, he vow'd to be her Debter
For many moe good turns then he would tell;
The least of which, this little Pleasure should excel.

The simple Maid did yield to him anon;
And eft him placed where he close might view
That never any saw, save onely one;
Who, for his Hire to so Fool-hardy due,
Was of his Hounds devour'd in Hunter's Hue.
Tho, as her manner was on sunny Day,
Diana, with her Nymphs about her, drew
To this sweet Spring; where, doffing her Array,
She bath'd her lovely Limbs, for *Jove* a likely Prey.

There *Faunus* saw that pleased much his eye,
And made his Heart to tickle in his Breast,
That for great Joy of somewhat he did spy,
He could him not contain in silent rest;
But breaking forth in Laughter loud, profest
His foolish Thought. O foolish *Faune* indeed,
That couldst not hold thy self so hidden blest,
But wouldest needs thine own Conceit areed:
Babblers unworthy been of so divine a Meed.

44–46

One gift in particular
did the trick: he knew
she longed to lie with
fellow-river Fanchin,
and so he, Faunus, undertook
to make this Fanchin
fall for her, and hard;
anything extra she desired,
consider it done, and all in trade
for this one good deed.

Innocent Molanna soon
gave in and got him front
row for a show no-one
had seen before, excepting
one, who paid when he
by his own hounds
was hunted down. Being
in a rut, Diana soon arrived
to bathe; the sort of centre
-fold that Jove enjoys.

Faun liked the view
and felt his heart - yes,
heart - lift as he saw
what he saw, and so
joyfully that he burst out
spontaneously into loud
laughter. Fool Faun!
you had to advertise
your fantasies. Blabber
-mouths don't prosper.

CANTO VI. 47—49

The Goddess, all abashed with that noise,
In haste forth started from the guilty Brook;
And running straight where-as she heard his Voice,
Enclos'd the Bush about, and there him took,
Like darred Lark; not daring up to look
On her whose sight before so much he sought.
Thence, forth they drew him by the Horns, and shook
Nigh all to pieces, that they left him nought;
And then into the open light they forth him brought.

Like as an Huswife, that with busy care
Thinks of her Dairy to make wondrous gain,
Finding whereas some wicked Beast unware
That breaks into her Dair'house, there doth drain
Her creaming Pans, and frustrate all her Pain;
Hath in some Snare or Gin set close behind,
Entrapped him, and caught into her train,
Then thinks what Punishment were best assign'd,
And thousand Deaths deviseth in her vengeful Mind:

So did *Diana* and her Maidens all
Use silly *Faunus*, now within their Bail:
They mock and scorn him, and him foul miscall;
Some by the Nose him pluck'd, some by the Tail,
And by his goatish Beard some did him hail:
Yet he (poor Soul) with patience all did bear;
For, nought against their wills might countervail:
Ne ought he said whatever he did hear;
But hanging down his Head, did like a Mome appear.

47–49

Startled, Diana rushed
out of the treacherous
waters, and by the echoing
bellowing, found him
in his illicit hide, and trapped
him like a dazzled lark there,
afraid suddenly to look her
in the eye, whom he had eyed
so avidly. They hauled him
by the antlers then, into the open.

When a spenser in her dairy,
dreaming the great returns
she'll get, discovers
vermin has destroyed
the store of white meats she'd
laid by, and wasted all her work,
she sets out snares, then spends
her leisure dreaming up
ingenious tortures
to dispatch the beasts.

That lovely gang dealt
likewise with this silly Faun:
made cruel fun of him, called
him disgusting, stupid, pulled
and poked him, and he
had no reply, no chance,
no matter what they said
to him, could do nothing at all
but feebly hang his head
and stand there like a dolt.

CANTO VI. 50—52

At length, when they had flouted him their fill,
They 'gan to cast what Penance him to give.
Some would have gelt him, but that same would spill
The Wood-Gods Breed, which must for ever live:
Others would through the River him have drive,
And ducked deep: but that seem'd Penance light;
But most agreed and did this Sentence give,
Him in Deer's skin to clad; and in that Plight,
To hunt him with their Hounds, himself save how he might.

But *Cynthia's* self, more angry than the rest,
Thought not enough, to punish him in sport,
And of her Shame to make a gamesom Jest;
But 'gan examine him in straighter sort,
Which of her Nymphs, or other close Consort,
Him thither brought, and her to him betray'd.
He, much affeard, to her confessed short,
That 'twas *Molanna* which her so bewray'd:
Then all attonce their Hands upon *Molanna* laid.

But him (according as they had decreed)
With a Deer's-Skin they cover'd, and then chac'd
With all their Hounds, that after him did speed;
But he more speedy, from them fled more fast
Than any Deer: so sore him Dread aghast.
They after follow'd all with shrill Outcry,
Shouting as they the Heavens would have brast:
That all the Woods and Dales, where he did fly,
Did ring again, and loud re-eccho to the Sky.

50–52

Tiring, they switched then to debate
his pain. *Castrate!* some said,
but might the breed of Wood
-Gods go extinct? *Drive*
to the river, then, and duck
him good! but, no, too lenient
for his fell deed! At last, consensus:
swaddle him in deer-hide, to outwit
his own hounds in the hunt:
set him against himself.

But the furious Goddess
repudiated all such superficial
measures, as trivializing her own
unfortunate embarrassment;
so, straight: *Who tipped the wink?*
He, fearing worse might follow,
put the finger on Molanna
as the guilty Nymph; and promptly
all her fair companions
turned their lovely fists on her.

They then covered him
with a hart fell, set
their hounds on him;
faster than any deer, he ran,
propelled by profound
terror, and the hunt came on,
pack sounding and resounding
as if to sunder Heaven;
and every wood and valley
reverberated with the cries.

CANTO VI. 53—55

So they him follow'd till they weary were;
When back returning to *Molann'* again,
They by Commandment of *Diana*, there
Her whelm'd with Stones. Yet *Faunus* (for her Pain)
Of her beloved *Fanchin* did obtain,
That her he would receive unto his Bed.
So now her Waves pass through a pleasant Plain,
Till with the *Fanchin* she her self do wed,
And (both combin'd) themselves in one faire River spred.

Nath'less *Diana*, full of Indignation,
Thenceforth abandon'd her delicious Brook;
In whose sweet Stream, before that bad Occasion,
So much Delight to bathe her Limbs she took:
Ne only her, but also quite forsook
All those fair Forests about *Arlo* hid,
And all that Mountain, which doth over-look
The richest Champain that may else be rid,
And the fair *Shure*, in which are thousand Salmons bred.

Them all, and all that she so dear did weigh,
Thenceforth she left; and parting from the Place,
Thereon an heavy hapless Curse did lay,
To weet, that Wolves, where she was wont to space,
Should harbour'd be, and all those Woods deface,
And Thieves should rob and spoil that Coast around.
Since which, those Woods, and all that goodly Chace,
Doth to this day with Wolves and Thieves abound:
Which too-too true that Land's In-dwellers since have found.

53–55

Then they turned back on
Molanna and, by order of Diana,
stoned her down with rocks.
But one thing Faunus
had delivered on was that
the Fanchin stream would
welcome her into his bed,
so now her waters spread
across the valley floor, and so
they lie now, one inclusive course.

Yet Diana fretted, took
a scunner against that
favourite stream of hers,
where she had loved
to bathe; likewise all features
thereabouts, damned
by association; Mount Arlo
too, though it surveys a golden
vale, and streams, in which
the salmon teem and breed.

All that, and all that other
she'd enjoyed, she left, and left
a curse behind her on the land:
wolves run where she had done,
marauders raid and seize hard
all increase. Since then, those woods,
and all that open ground, are thick
with vermin, dense with untold
promiscuous varieties, as those
who've lived there can attest.

CANTO VII 1—3

Ah! whither dost thou now, thou greater Muse,
Me from these Woods and pleasing Forests bring?
And my frail Spirit (that doth oft refuse
This too high Flight, unfit for her weak Wing)
Lift up aloft, to tell of Heaven's King
(Thy sovereign Sire) his fortunate Success,
And Victory, in bigger Notes to sing,
Which he obtain'd against that *Titaness*,
That him of Heaven's Empire sought to dispossess.

Yet sith I needs must follow thy Behest,
Do thou my weaker Wit with Skill inspire,
Fit for this turn; and in my feeble Breast
Kindle fresh Sparks of that immortal Fire,
Which learned Minds inflameth with Desire
Of heavenly things: for who but thou alone,
That art yborn of Heaven and heavenly Sire,
Can tell things doen in Heaven so long ygone:
So far past Memory of Man that may be known?

Now, at the time that was before agreed,
The Gods assembled all on *Arlo* Hill;
As well those that are sprung of heavenly Seed,
As those that all the other World do fill,
And rule both Sea and Land unto their will:
Only th'infernal Powers might not appear;
As well for Horrour of their Count'nance ill,
As for th'unruly Fiends which they did fear;
Yet *Pluto* and *Proserpina* were present there.

56–58

Turn now from these easy tales
of woods and streams. (I'm not sure
I can sustain this other history
of Heaven, and the lucky verdict
for its King; a win like that deserves
a bigger buzz than I can magic
up, since it's not everyday a Titaness
attempting Heaven is repulsed.

But if I must, I must: Muse, tune
my song, and fit me for the task
ahead; kindle me up again, let me blaze
when it comes to matters theological,
since you yourself, oh Muse, being sired
in Heaven, must know all the scoop,
and so can fill my failing verse with high
events out of the gutters of prehistory.)

So, to proceed: at the set hour the Gods
all got together on Mount Arlo; not just
the Deities of superior caste, but also
Gods of Water and of Land. Only the fiends
of Hell were denied entry, as calculated
to offend a delicate sensibility;
Pluto and Proserpina alone
of that class made the cut.

CANTO VII. 4—6

And thither also came all other Creatures,
Whatever Life or Motion do retain,
According to their sundry kinds of Features;
That *Arlo* scarsely could them all contain;
So full they filled every Hill and Plain:
And had not *Nature's* Sergeant (that is, *Order*)
Them well disposed by his busy Pain,
And raunged farre abroad in every Border,
They would have caused much Confusion and Disorder.

Then forth issu'd (great Goddess) great Dame *Nature*,
With goodly Port and gracious Majesty;
Being far greater and more tall of Stature
Than any of the Gods or Powers on high:
Yet certes by her Face and Phisnomy,
Whether she Man or Woman inly were,
That could not any Creature well descry:
For, with a Veil that wimpled every where,
Her Head and Face was hid, that mote to none appear.

That some do say was so by Skill deviz'd,
To hide the Terrour of her uncouth Hue
From mortal Eyes that should be sore agriz'd;
For that her Face did like a Lion shew,
That Eye of Wight could not endure to view:
But others tell that it so beauteous was,
And round about such Beams of Splendor threw,
That it the Sun a thousand times did pass,
Ne could be seen, but like an Image in a Glass.

59–61

The rest of animate creation came too,
so many and so various that Arlo, fit
to burst, struggled to contain them all,
and they spilled over onto every adjacent
ground, and had not Order, Nature's bright
receptionist, guided them into their
allocated places, and sweet-talked throughout,
it would have been one god-awful mess.

Then great Nature showed herself;
majestic, and with truly excellent
deportment, greater by far than any
of the other Gods, and taller too.
But whether she was really male
or female, no-one knew for sure,
because she wore a hood, no matter
how she moved, covered her face.

Some say that was a feigned effect; eyes
of mortal creatures couldn't tolerate
the terror of something so bizarre; her face,
if anything, resembling a lion, but of a sort
too horrible to be endured by human
eye; yet others say it was so beautiful, its glory
greater than a thousand suns, that it
would likewise blind if looked at straight.

CANTO VII. 7—9

That well may seemen true: for well I ween
    That this same day, when she on *Arlo* sat,
    Her Garment was so bright and wondrous sheen,
    That my frail Wit cannot devize to what
    It to compare, nor find like Stuff to that,
    As those three sacred *Saints*, though else most wise,
    Yet on Mount *Thabor* quite their Wits forgat,
    When they their glorious Lord in strange Disguise
Transfigur'd saw; his Garments so did daze their Eyes.

In a fair Plain upon an equal Hill,
    She placed was in a Pavilion;
    Not such as Craftsmen by their idle Skill
    Are wont for Princes States to fashion:
    But th'Earth her self of her own Motion,
    Out of her fruitful Bosom made to grow
    Most dainty Trees; that, shooting up anon,
    Did seem to bow their blooming Heads full low,
For Homage unto her, and like a Throne did show.

So hard it is for any living Wight,
    All her Array and Vestiments to tell,
    That old Dan *Geffrey* (in whose gentle Spright
    The pure Well-head of Poesy did dwell)
    In his *Fowls Parley* durst not with it mell,
    But it transfer'd to *Alane*, who he thought
    Had in his *Plaint of Kinds* describ'd it well:
    Which who will read set forth so as it ought,
Go seek he out that *Alane* where he may be sought.

62–64

Both may be true, but this I know,
that when she settled on Arlo's
plateau, her habit was so bright, so strange,
I have no words for it, no metaphors to make
that an intelligible stuff; so just hear this:
when Christ transfigured upon Thabor's top,
his saints lost their sense, his habit
stunned their eyes, as hers my wit.

As princes often have pavilions
crafted for them by the finest hands,
so Nature, too, has hers, though one not
made by any human hand, but rather
a pavilion originated out of her rich self,
her own luxuriance; fine-timbered trees
that sprouted instantly, and then dipped
canopies as to confect a throne.

Her clothing, though, surpassed human
description, so old Chaucer (whose spirit
was a fountain-head of verse) was quite savvy
not to try it when he came to write
his *Parliament of Fowls*, but instead let Alan
have his say, who in his *Plaint of Kinds* had it
down to a T, so if you want the best account,
go get yourself a copy of Alan's report.

CANTO VII. 10—12

And all the earth far underneath her Feet
Was dight with Flow'rs, that voluntary grew
Out of the Ground, and sent forth Odours sweet;
Ten thousand more of sundry Scent and Hue,
That might delight the Smell, or please the View:
The which, the Nymphs, from all the Brooks thereby
Had gathered, they at her Foot-stool threw;
That richer seem'd than any Tapestry,
That Princes Bow'rs adorn with painted Imagery.

And *Mole* himself, to honour her the more,
Did deck himself in freshest fair Attire,
And his high Head, that seemeth always hoar
With harden'd Frosts of former Winter's Ire,
He with an oaken Girlond now did tire,
As if the Love of some new Nymph late seen,
Had in him kindled youthful fresh Desire,
And made him change his gray Attire to green:
Ah! gentle *Mole*, such Joyance hath thee well beseen!

Was never so great Joyance since the day,
That all the Gods whilome assembled were
On *Hæmus'* Hill in their divine Array,
To celebrate the solemn bridal Chear
Twixt *Peleeus*, and Dame *Thetis* pointed there
Where *Phoebus'* self, that God of Poets hight,
They say did sing the spousal Hymn full clear,
That all the Gods were ravish'd with Delight
Of his celestial Song, and Musick's wondrous Might.

65–67

Underfoot, the surface of the Earth
was spread with fragrant flowers,
that grew spontaneously up
out of the ground; and the Nymphs
scattered at her feet innumerable more
varieties, both scented and attractive
to the eye, plucked from near streams,
all more perplexed than any royal tapestry.

That mountain range we know as Mole,
was done up too in freshest finery,
and even his head, grizzled
and scarred ordinarily with frosts,
put on a garland of green oak,
as if he'd hoped to pull some pretty
Nymph that made him lust again, and so
had changed from his familiar grey to green.

There never had been such a gig
since that day the costumed Gods
all gathered on Mount Haemus
for the nuptials of Peleus and his bride,
Thetis, and that class act,
Phoebus A himself, crooned
out the wedding hymn, and made
his godly audience swoon.

CANTO VII. 13—15

This Great Grandmother of all Creatures bred,
Great *Nature*, ever young yet full of eld,
Still moving, yet unmoved from her Sted,
Unseen of any, yet of all beheld,
Thus sitting in her Throne, as I have teld,
Before her came Dame *Mutability*;
And being low before her Presence feld,
With meek Obeysance and Humility,
Thus 'gan her plaintiff Plea, with Words to amplify:

To thee, O greatest Goddess! only great,
An humble Suppliant loe! I lowly fly,
Seeking for Right, which I of thee entreat;
Who Right to all dost deal indifferently,
Damning all Wrong and tortious Injury,
Which any of thy creatures do to other
(Oppressing them with Pow'r, unequally)
Sith of them all thou art the equal Mother,
And knittest each to each, as Brother unto Brother.

To thee therefore of this same *Jove* I' plain,
And of his Fellow-Gods that fain to be,
That challenge to themselves the whole World's Reign;
Of which the greatest part is due to me,
And Heaven it self by Heritage in Fee:
For Heaven and Earth I both alike do deem,
Sith Heaven and Earth are both alike to thee;
And Gods no more than Men thou dost esteem:
For, even the Gods to thee, as Men to Gods do seem.

68–70

Before this enthroned judge,
this Grandam of all living
entities, young yet full of age, still
moving though herself unmoved,
invisible while in full view,
came plaintive Mutability,
who bowed respectfully,
then launched her case:

Before you, Supreme Goddess, I,
humble though importunate,
appear to pray you deal me
impartial Justice, correcting
here another injury done by strength
to weakness, as you are Mother
equally to all, and so bind each
to each, as one Brother to another.

Here I arraign this Jove and his
co-Gods, who claim the universe
as theirs, though most of it
- even Heaven itself - is mine,
as my inheritance. And like you, I
recognize no difference between
Gods and men, since to you the Gods
are puny as are men to Gods.

CANTO VII. 16—18

Then weigh, O Sovereign Goddess, by what Right
These Gods do claim the World's whole Sovereignty;
And that is only due unto thy Might,
Arrogate to themselves ambitiously:
As for the Gods own Principality,
Which *Jove* usurpes unjustly; that to be
My Heritage, *Jove's* self cannot deny,
From my Great Grandsire *Titan*, unto me
Deriv'd by due Descent, as is well known to thee.

Yet maugre *Jove*, and all his Gods beside,
I do possess the World's most Regiment;
As, if ye please it into Parts divide,
And every Part's Inholders to convent,
Shall to your Eyes appear incontinent.
And first, the Earth (great Mother of us all)
That only seems unmov'd and permanent,
And unto *Mutability* not thrall;
Yet is she chang'd in part, and eke in general.

For, all that from her springs, and is ybred,
However fair it flourish for a time,
Yet see we soon decay; and, being dead,
To turn again unto their earthly Slime:
Yet out of their Decay and mortal Crime,
We daily see new Creatures to arise;
And of their Winter spring another Prime,
Unlike in Form, and chang'd by strange Disguise:
So turn they still about, and change in restless wise.

71–73

Assess the grounds on which these
Gods claim lordship of the world,
laying claim even to things and deeds
which are your doings alone, my Lord.
As for their home turf, Heaven, Jove
can't deny he stole it from my Father's
Father, Titan, though all know
it is my legacy as lineal heir.

So much for Goddish trivia. Let's move
to consequential things: the world's root
rule is mine. If you'll accept
evidence from every element,
take first our universal Mother Earth,
who seems final and most fixed,
immutable, and yet in every part
and as a whole, throughout is changed.

All that springs from Earth flickers
a while: it flourishes, then falls
rotting back to filth; and this decay
generates in turn a new ten thousand
things; they flower, their winter kills them,
but their spring succeeds, and they
return, unrecognizably, to change
and change and change again.

CANTO VII. 19—21

As for her Tenants; that is, Man and Beasts,
The Beasts we daily see massacred die,
As Thralls and Vassals unto Mens Beheasts:
And Men themselves do change continually,
From Youth to Eld, from Wealth to Poverty,
From Good to Bad, from Bad to Worst of all.
Ne do their Bodies only flit and fly;
But eke their Minds (which they immortal call)
Still change and vary Thoughts, as new Occasions fall.

Ne is the Water in more constant case;
Whether those same on high, or these below:
For, th'Ocean moveth stil, from place to place;
And every River still doth ebb and flow:
Ne any Lake, that seems most still and slow,
Ne Pool so small, that can his Smoothness hold,
When any Wind doth under Heaven blow;
With which the Clouds are also toss'd and roll'd;
Now like great Hills, and straight, like Sluices, them unfold.

So likewise are all watry living Wights
Still toss'd and turned with continual Change
Never abiding in their stedfast Plights.
The Fish, still floating, do at random range,
And never rest; but evermore exchange
Their dwelling Places, as the Streams them carry:
Ne have the watry Fowls a certain Grange,
Wherein to rest, ne in one stead do tarry;
But flitting still do fly, and still their Places vary.

74–76

Consider man and beast, that lodge
in Earth: those beasts are slaughtered
ceaselessly at whim, while men, change
drives from youth to age, from wealth
to poverty, from best to good to bad to worst
of all, and as their bodies slip from one
stage to the next, their minds too,
fluctuate from thought to thought.

There's no greater constancy in water,
above us or below. See how unsteady
still the ocean is, and always on the go,
and how still estuaries ebb and flow;
search out where water seems most still
and slow, a lake, say, or a little pool, and see
how, stormed, all smoothness goes,
as the clouds mount, and empty like a sluice.

Still spun in an incessant turbine,
no sea-beasts enjoy any stead
-fastness. Fish float, but still can't
rest or last in just one place, but move
always as the currents move;
as for the water-fowl, their flats
and sands offer no stand, but they must
flutter always in the shifting winds.

CANTO VII. 22—24

Next is the Air: which who feels not by Sense
(For, of all Sense it is the middle Mean)
To flit still? and with subtle Influence
Of his thin Spirit, all Creatures to maintain,
In State of Life? O weak Life! that does lean
On thing so tickle as th'unsteady Air;
Which every hour is chang'd, and alter'd clean
With every Blast that bloweth foul or fair:
The fair doth it prolong; the foul doth it impair.

Therein the Changes infinite behold,
Which to her Creatures every minute chaunce:
Now boiling hot; straight friezing deadly cold:
Now fair Sun-shine, that makes all skip and daunce:
Straight, bitter Storms and baleful Countenance,
That makes them all to shiver and to shake:
Rain, Hail, and Snow do pay them sad Penance,
And dreadful Thunder-Claps (that make them quake)
With Flames and flashing Lights that thousand Changes make.

Last is the Fire: which, though it live for ever,
Ne can be quenched quite; yet, every day,
We see his Parts, so soon as they do sever,
To lose their Heat, and shortly to decay;
So, makes himself his own consuming Prey.
Ne any living Creatures doth he breed:
But all, that are of others bred, doth slay;
And, with their Death, his cruel Life doth feed;
Nought leaving, but their barren Ashes, without Seed.

77–79

Take next the air: no trusting it.
Haven't you felt its endless stop, start, stop?
There's never any dwelling in it, yet
it's this thin influence sustains all entities
in life, though life must be a very
flimsy thing if it depend on anything
so unstable as this air that goes
from fair to foul with the least gust.

Change follows change in swift
successions of catastrophes: first
scalding heat torments poor beasts,
then lethal cold; now sun for sport,
next, storm's a total killjoy, leaves
them shuddering; they get rain, hail,
and blizzards for their pains, till seismic
shocks mark cataclysmic change.

Finally, that inextinguishable, Fire,
is no exception: see, how his
quick sparks fly and fall, then dull
and cool; savagely, he hunts down
and devours himself; he breeds no life
but is a cruel end to others, as he fattens
on their death, til nothing's left
but ashes, dust, and arid residues.

CANTO VII. 25—27

Thus, all these four (the which the Ground-work be
Of all the World, and of all living Wights)
To thousand sorts of *Change* we subject see:
Yet are they chang'd (by other wondrous Slights)
Into themselves, and lose their native Mights;
The Fire to Air, and th'Air to Water sheer,
And Water into Earth ; yet Water fights
With Fire, and Air with Earth approaching near:
Yet all are in one Body, and as one appear.

So, in them all reigns *Mutability*;
However these, that Gods themselves do call,
Of them do claim the Rule and Sovereignty:
As, *Vesta*, of the Fire Eterneal;
Vulcan, of this, with us so usual;
Ops, of the Earth; and *Juno,* of the Air;
Neptune, of Seas; and Nymphs, of Rivers all.
For all those Rivers to me subject are:
And all the rest, which they usurp, be all my Share.

Which to approven true, as I have told,
Vouchsafe, O Goddess! to thy Presence call
The rest which do the World in Being hold;
As, Times and Seasons of the Year that fall:
Of all the which, demand in general,
Or judge thy self, by Verdict of thine Eye,
Whether to me they are not subject all.
Nature did yield thereto; and by and by
Bade *Order* call them all, before her Majesty.

80–82

This fundamental foursome, then,
themselves suffer ten thousand
tricks of change, and intermix,
losing all specificity: fire slips
to air, air thickens into water, water
turns to earth; yet fire struggles
against water, air against earth;
and all are inextricable contraries.

So I, Mutability, am paramount
in all, and yet, these petty self
-proclaimed Divinities, vie
at a remove, split their elemental
loot, pretending to hold things
settled and quiesced; yet things stay
disquieted, and it is I,
not they, am fluent in them all.

To clinch my case, Judge Goddess,
condescend to call up those bum
-bailiffs of your writ: interrogate
the Terms that section and distrain
our Time, whose side they're on,
then let that evidence do justice
to my claim.
So Nature did
command: *approach and testify!*

CANTO VII. 28—30

So, forth issu'd the Seasons of the Year;
First, lusty *Spring*, all dight in Leaves of Flow'rs
That freshly budded and new Bloosms did bear
(In which a thousand Birds had built their Bow'rs
That sweetly sung, to call forth Paramours:)
And in his Hand a Javelin he did bear,
And on his Head (as fit for warlike Stours)
A gilt engraven Morion he did wear;
That as some did him love, so others did him fear.

Then came the jolly *Summer*, being dight
In a thin silken Cassock colour'd green,
That was unlined all, to be more light:
And on his Head a Girlond well beseen
He wore, from which as he had chauffed been
The Sweat did drop; and in his Hand he bore
A Bow and Shafts, as he in Forest green
Had hunted late the Libbard or the Boar,
And now would bathe his Limbs, with Labour heated sore.

Then came the *Autumn* all in Yellow clad,
As though he joyed in his plenteous Store,
Laden with Fruits that made him laugh, full glad
That he had banish'd Hunger, which to-fore
Had by the Belly oft him pinched sore.
Upon his Head a Wreath that was enroll'd
With Ears of Corn of every sort, he bore:
And in his Hand a Sickle he did hold,
To reap the ripen'd Fruits, the which the Earth had yold.

83–85

The seasons were first up:

Spring, primped
in blossoms and small
songbirds' nests, gripped
a javelin, switched
suddenly from smile
to frown to smile again.

Summer then sweated in,
hot from the hunt,
though dressed in a fine
green mantle, and with
bow and several
arrows in his grip.

Autumn came next,
costumed in yellow,
radiating fullness and good
fellowship, a sickle
in his hand, to reap
the ripe yield of the Earth.

CANTO VII. 31—33

Lastly, came *Winter* clothed all in Frize,
Chattering his Teeth for Cold that did him chill,
Whilst on his hoary Beard his Breath did freeze;
And the dull Drops that from his purpled Bill,
As from a Limbeck did adown distill.
In his right Hand a tipped Staff he held,
With which his feeble Steps he stayed still:
For he was faint with Cold, and weak with Eld;
That scarce his loosed Limbs he able was to weld.

These, marching softly, thus in order went,
And after them, the Months all riding came;
First, sturdy *March*, with Brows full sternly bent,
And armed strongly, rode upon a Ram,
The same which over *Hellespontus* swam:
Yet in his Hand a Spade he also hent,
And in a Bag all sorts of Seeds ysame,
Which on the Earth he strowed as he went,
And fill'd her Womb with fruitful Hope of Nourishment.

Next came fresh *April* full of Lustyhead,
And wanton as a Kid, whose Horn new buds;
Upon a Bull he rode, the same which led
Europa floating through th'*Argolick* Floods:
His Horns were gilden all with golden Studs,
And garnished with Garlands, goodly dight
Of all the fairest Flowr's and freshest Buds
Which th'Earth brings forth, and wet he seem'd in sight
With Waves, through which he waded for his Love's Delight.

86–88

Winter hindmost, in a coat
of frieze, his teeth
chattering with cold,
breath white on beard,
and bright nose snuffling
as he shuffled through.

Next up, the months in sequence processed by:

March, heavily armed
and frowning, rode
a Ram like that which swam
the Hellespont;
with spade and seed
he sowed the fertile Earth.

April, lusty, playful
as a kidling goat, bestrode
the Bull that bore
Europa off; horns starred
with gold, still drenched,
and decked with buds.

CANTO VII. 34—36

Then came fair *May*, the fairest Maid on ground,
Deck'd all with Dainties of her Season's Pride,
And throwing Flow'rs out of her Lap around:
Upon two Brethrens Shoulders she did ride,
The Twins of *Leda*; which on either side
Supported her like to their sovereign Queen.
Lord! how all Creatures laugh'd, when her they spy'd,
And leap'd and daunc'd as they had ravish'd been!
And *Cupid's* self about her flutter'd all in green.

And after her, came jolly *June*, array'd
All in green Leaves, as he a Player were;
Yet in his time, he wrought as well as play'd,
That by his Plough-yrons mote right well appear:
Upon a Crab he rode, that him did bear
With crooked crawling Steps an uncouth Pace,
And backward yode, as Bargemen wont to fare
Bending their Force contrary to their Face,
Like that ungracious Crew which feigns demurest Grace.

Then came hot *July* boiling like to Fire,
That all his Garments he had cast away;
Upon a Lion raging yet with Ire
He boldly rode and made him to obey:
It was the Beast that whylome did forray
The *Nemaean* Forest, till th'*Amphytrionide*
Him slew, and with his Hide did him array:
Behind his Back a Sithe, and by his Side
Vnder his Belt he bore a Sickle circling wide.

89–91

May, prettied up
with flowers and berries
that she strewed; Twins
Gemini supported her,
and all creatures, Cupid
too, cavorted to see.

June, accessorized
in leaves like Savage Man,
but with ploughshares
by his side, sprawled on a Crab
that shifted back and forward
like an awkward guest.

July, stripped for heat,
straddled the Lion
that Hercules
subdued, and bore
his tools of trade:
a sickle and a scythe.

CANTO VII. 37—39

The sixth was *August*, being rich array'd
In Garment all of Gold down to the ground;
Yet rode he not, but led a lovely Maid
Forth by the Lilly Hand, the which was crown'd
With Ears of Corn, and full her Hand was found:
That was the righteous Virgin, which of old
Liv'd here on Earth, and plenty made abound;
But, after Wrong was lov'd and Justice sold,
She left th'unrighteous World and was to Heaven extol'd.

Next him, *September* marched eke on foot;
Yet was he heavy laden with the Spoil
Of Harvest's Riches, which he made his Boot,
And him enrich'd with Bounty of the Soil:
In his one hand, as fit for Harvest's Toil,
He held a Knife-hook; and in th'other hand
A pair of Weights, with which he did assoil
Both more and less, where it in doubt did stand,
And equal gave to each, as Justice duly scann'd.

Then came *October* full of merry Glee:
For, yet his Noul was totty of the Must,
Which he was treading in the Wine-Fats see,
And of the joyous Oil, whose gentle Gust
Made him so frolick and so full of Lust:
Upon a dreadful Scorpion he did ride,
The same which by *Diana's* doom unjust
Slew great *Orion*; and eke by his Side
He had his Ploughing-Share, and Coulter ready ty'd.

92–94

August draped in golden
cloth, unmounted, led
a maiden out, who, laden
down with corn, having abjured
the evil world, lives on
exalted in the stars.

September followed, bowed
with a heavy harvest load;
he held a sickle and a set
of scales, so could discriminate
the greater from the less
and warrant Justice done.

October, tipsy with new
wine, lusty with oils,
rode by on that same
Scorpion stung Orion
to his death; his ploughing
tackle dangled alongside.

CANTO VII. 40—42

Next was *November*, he full gross and fat,
As fed with Lard, and that right well might seem;
For, he had been a fatting Hogs of late,
That yet his Brows with Sweat did reek and steem,
And yet the Season was full sharp and breem;
In planting eke he took no small delight:
Whereon he rode, not easy was to deem;
For it a dreadful *Centaur* was in sight,
The seed of *Saturn* and fair *Nais, Chiron* hight,

And after him, came next the chill *December:*
Yet he through merry Feasting which he made,
And great Bonfires, did not the Cold remember;
His Saviour's Birth his mind so much did glad:
Upon a shaggy-bearded Goat he rode,
The same wherewith Dan *Jove* in tender Years,
They say, was nourisht by th'*I[d]ean* Maid;
And in his hand a broad deep Bowl he bears;
Of which, he freely drinks an Health to all his Peers.

Then came old *January*, wrapped well
In many Weeds to keep the Cold away;
Yet did he quake and quiver like to quell,
And blow his Nails to warm them if he may;
For, they were numb'd with holding all the day
An Hatchet keen, with which he felled Wood,
And from the Trees did lop the needless Spray;
Upon an huge great Earth-pot Stean he stood;
From whose wide Mouth, there flowed forth the Roman Flood.

95–97

November, larded up,
sweated profusely
in the turbulent air; he had
a Centaur saddled, Ciron
by name, one foaled out
of a Nymph, Saturn the sire.

December was too festive
to observe his cold,
as, marking the Nativity
of his Lord, he rode the Goat
that nourished infant Jove,
toasting our health.

January stood coated up,
yet blew his frozen fists
for cold, numb from long hours
of pollarding; beneath
his feet, an Urn, that poured
great inundation out.

CANTO VII. 43—45

And lastly, came cold *February*, sitting
In an old Waggon, for he could not ride;
Drawn of two Fishes for the Season fitting,
Which through the Flood before did softly slide
And swim away: yet had he by his side
His Plough and Harness fit to till the Ground,
And Tools to prune the Trees, before the pride
Of hasting Prime did make them burgein round:
So past the twelve Months forth, and their due places found.

And after these, there came the *Day* and *Night*,
Riding together both with equal pace,
Th' one on a Palfrey black, the other white;
But *Night* had cover'd her uncomely Face
With a black Veil, and held in hand a Mace,
On top whereof the Moon and Stars were pight,
And Sleep and Darkness round about did trace:
But *Day* did bear, upon his Scepter's hight,
The goodly Sun, encompast all with Beames bright.

Then came the *Hours*, fair daughters of high *Jove*,
And timely *Night*, the which were all endu'd
With wondrous Beauty fit to kindle Love;
But they were Virgins all, and Love eschew'd,
That might forslack the charge to them fore-shew'd
By mighty *Jove*; who did them Porters make
Of Heaven's Gate (whence all the Gods issu'd)
Which they did daily watch, and nightly wake
By even turnes, ne ever did their Charge forsake.

98–100

February, last, sat in a cart
two fishes dragged along,
borne by that flood; a plough
and harness at his side,
and pruning tools. And that
made up the twelve.

Next witnesses were Day
and Night, their mounts
abreast, one a true black,
the other white; Night,
her unfavour perfectly
obscured, brandished
a mace embellished
with the moon and stars,
and Sleep and Darkness
hovered near;
Day bore the bright
and wholesome sun.

And then the Hours,
daughters of Jove
and Night, each easy
on the eye, though none
of them had time
for love, being far
too occupied
with their appointed
task: to watch in turn
at Heaven's Gate, and usher
through the Gods
as they went in and out.

CANTO VII. 46—48

And after all came *Life*, and lastly *Death*:
  Death with most grim and griesly Visage seen,
  Yet is he nought but parting of the Breath;
  Ne ought to see, but like a Shade to ween,
  Unbodied, unsoul'd, unheard, unseen.
  But *Life* was like a faire young lusty Boy,
  Such as they feign *Dan Cupid* to have been,
  Full of delightful Health and lively Joy.
Deckt all with Flowers, and Wings of Gold fit to employ.

When these were past, thus 'gan the *Titaness*;
  Lo! mighty Mother, now be Judg and say,
  Whether in all thy Creatures more or less
  CHANGE doth not reign & bear the greatest sway;
  For, who sees not, that *Time* on all doth prey?
  But *Times* do change and move continually;
  So nothing here long standeth in one stay:
  Wherefore, this lower World who can deny
But to be subject still to *Mutability?*

Then thus 'gan *Jove*; Right true it is, that these
  And all things else that under Heaven dwell
  Are chaung'd of *Time*, who doth them all disseize
  Of Being : But, who is it (to me tell)
  That *Time* himself doth move and still compel
  To keep his course? Is not that namely we
  Which pour that Vertue from our heavenly Cell,
  That moves them all, and makes them changed be?
So them we Gods do rule, and in them also thee.

101–103

After these, Time's
divisions, followed Life,
then Death, who, grim
and hateful as he seems,
is only a last breath
-lessness, an unheard,
unbodied, unsouled, unseen
shade; but Life was lusty
as young Cupid was,
all rude health and joy,
wreathed in flowers,
and imped with golden wings.

This done, the Titaness addressed
great Nature: *Judge, Mighty Mother:*
throughout all your varied bestiary,
isn't it Change predates? Doesn't
Time carve up the lot of them? Zilch
stands exempt. I put it to you, then,
as undeniable, that in this gross transitory
world it's Mutability who's boss.

So, Jove rejoined: *Without question,*
Time does injury to all things under Heaven,
and dispossesses them of Being; true,
Time is urgent, but who urges Time? Who
else but Gods, that though remote can
send our agent to compel all things
out of their dwelling; make, from disaster,
opportunity? We are the Lords of Change.

CANTO VII. 49—51

To whom, thus *Mutability*: The things
Which we see not how they are mov'd and sway'd,
Ye may attribute to your selves as Kings,
And say they by your secret Power are made:
But what we see not, who shall us persuade?
But were they so, as ye them feign to be,
Mov'd by your Might, and order'd by your Aid;
Yet what if I can prove, that even ye
Your selves are likewise chang'd, and subject unto me?

And first, concerning her that is the first,
Even you fair *Cynthia*, whom so much ye make
Jove's dearest Darling, she was bred and nurst
On *Cynthus'* Hill, whence she her Name did take;
Then is she mortal born, how-so ye crake:
Besides, her Face and Countenance every day
We changed see, and sundry Forms partake,
Now horn'd, now round, now bright, now brown and grey:
So that *as changeful as the Moon* Men use to say.

Next, *Mercury*, who though he less appear
To change his Hue, and always seem as one;
Yet, he his Course doth alter every Year,
And is of late far out of order gone:
So *Venus* eke, that goodly Paragon,
Though fair all Night, yet is she dark all Day;
And *Phoebus'* self, who lightsome is alone,
Yet is he oft eclipsed by the way,
And fills the darkned World with Terror and Dismay.

104–106

Then Mutability: *You claim*
to own this agency that makes
things move and change. Maybe
you do, or maybe not. Who
knows? But even grant the case
is as you say: allow me prove
you also slide from self
to self, and are so my subjects too.

First things first: This Lady Moon, this
Cynthia, was reared and named from Cynthus,
a terrestrial hill; spin it how you want,
she's low, this Lady, and of mortal stock.
And, watch how her expression shifts
from day to day: brightness turns dark,
broad thins, full empties out anew,
as she goes through another phase.

That cliché that men use is functional:
'As fickle as the Moon'. And Mercury,
constant by comparison, has his prank years
(like this our last). Then Venus: brightest
Goddess in the night, yet dark all day. Some
beauty, she! Can you rely even on Sun himself?
He's radiant most days, but when that's
eclipsed, what fills the void? Terror and dismay.

CANTO VII. 52—54

Now *Mars* that valiant Man is changed most:
For he some times so far runs out of square,
That he his way doth seem quite to have lost,
And clean without his usual Sphere to fare;
That even these Star-gazers stonisht are
At sight thereof, and damn their lying Books:
So likewise, grim Sir *Saturn* oft doth spare
His stern Aspect, and calm his crabbed Looks:
So many turning Cranks these have, so many Crooks.

But you Dan *Jove*, that only constant are,
And King of all the rest, as ye do claim,
Are you not subject eke to this Misfare?
Then let me ask you this withouten blame,
Where were ye born? some say in *Crete* by Name,
Others in *Thebes*, and others other-where;
But wheresoever they comment the same,
They all consent that ye begotten were,
And born here in this World, ne other can appear.

Then are ye mortal born, and thrall to me,
Unless the Kingdom of the Sky ye make
Immortal, and unchangeable to be;
Besides, that Power and Vertue which ye spake,
That ye here work, doth many Changes take,
And your own Natures change: for, each of you
That Vertue have, or this or that to make,
Is checkt and changed from his Nature true,
By other's Opposition or obliquid View.

107–109

Mars displays his steadfast military
occupation, sure! And yet he staggers
like he's lost abroad, causing
wise men to doubt their epheremides
and curse them now for flagrant lies;
while Saturn, most notorious for grim,
though on occasion he turn kind,
is much too unpredictable to trust.

And you, King Jove, that set yourself
up as top dog for constancy, don't you
never flit, or find you're lost? And, tell me,
without prejudice, where were you born?
Some allege Crete, some Thebes, yet others
say yet some other place. They may
squabble as to that, this they agree:
you were spawned in a low world.

Then you're mere mortal too, and mine,
unless you've sourced for Sky some super
extra heavy-duty neverfade preservative. And,
anyway, that influence you claim you have
down here, it also suffers change,
as do all your Goddy natures: you each
have your own influence, yet that is torqued
from true, each by another's force.

CANTO VII. 55—57

Besides, the sundry Motions of your Spheres,
So sundry ways and fashions as Clerks feign,
Some in short space, and some in longer Years;
What is the same but Alteration plain?
Only the starry Sky doth still remain:
Yet do the Stars and Signs therein still move,
And even it self is mov'd, as Wizards sain.
But all that moveth, doth Mutation love:
Therefore both you and them to me I subject prove.

Then since within this wide great *Universe*
Nothing doth firm and permanent appear,
But all things tost and turned by transverse:
What then should lett, but I aloft should rear
My Trophy, and from all the Triumph bear?
Now judge then (O thou greatest Goddess true!)
According as thy self dost see and hear,
And unto me addoom that is my Due;
That is the Rule of all, all being rul'd by you.

So having ended, silence long ensu'd,
Ne *Nature* to or fro spake for a space,
But with firm Eyes affixt, the ground still view'd.
Meanwhile, all Creatures, looking in her Face,
Expecting th'end of this so doubtful Case,
Did hang in long suspence what would ensue,
To whether side should fall the Sovereign Place.
At length, she looking up with chearful view,
The Silence brake, and gave her Doom in Speeches few.

110–112

Hear me out! Your various orbits have
each their own periods and trajectories,
some brief, some long. You call
that constancy? Only the outermost
integument of stars survives our argument,
yet stars and houses still slide even there,
and space itself is ruined. In short, all
that moves commotion loves, and it is mine.

Note, then: there are no fixtures
in this whole vast universe; all furniture
is slippery. So vindicate my cause, let
verdict be mine! Adjudicate then,
Goddess Judge. You've seen and heard
my true submission; deliver me your ruling
and ajudge my due to me: my fundamental rule
is paramount, all subject to your rule.

Nature fell mute, seemed to have lost
ability to speak, her gaze fixed
on the ground. The court audience
watched her face, wondering at the end
of this uncertain case, how she'd
come down. At last, she lifted up
her head, and smiled; then, breaking
silence, she proclaimed her writ.

CANTO VII. 58—59

I well consider all that ye have said,
　And find that all things Stedfastness do hate
　And changed be: yet being rightly weigh'd
　They are not changed from their first Estate;
　But by their Change their Being do dilate:
　And turning to themselves at length again,
　Do work their own Perfection so by Fate:
　Then over them Change doth not rule and reign;
But they reign over Change, and do their States maintain.

Cease therefore, Daughter, further to aspire,
　And thee content thus to be rul'd by me:
　For thy Decay thou seekst by thy Desire;
　But time shall come that all shall changed be,
　And from thenceforth, none no more Change shall see.
　So was the *Titaness* put down and whist,
　And *Jove* confirm'd in his imperial See.
　Then was that whole Assembly quite dismist,
And *Nature's* self did vanish, whither no Man wist.

113–114

I have heard and given thought
to everything put before me, and I find
truly all things hate fixity, and so see
themselves translated: yet, properly
considered, they are not so radically
changed as to be utterly divorced
from what they were, but rather are
extended in themselves, accommodating
their variety as they grow. Therefore
I say that Change does not govern them,
but that they govern change,
and so are settled in themselves.

So, Daughter, limit aspiration,
be satisfied to be overruled
by me; else your own ruin
you desire. A time will come when all
things will be changed, and after that
none no more Change shall see. Just so,
the Titaness was quenched,
quiesced, and Jove confirmed
in his imperial authority. That was
the whole deal done. The assembly
was dismissed, and Nature
gone, underground again.

CANTO VIII. 1—2

When I bethink me on that Speech whylear,
Of *Mutability*, and well it weigh;
Me seems, that though she all unworthy were
Of the Heav'ns Rule; yet very sooth to say,
In all things else she bears the greatest sway.
Which makes me loath this state of Life so tickle,
And Love of things so vain to cast away;
Whose flowring Pride, so fading and so fickle,
Short *Time* shall soon cut down with his consuming Sickle.

Then 'gin I think on that which Nature said,
Of that same time when no more *Change* shall be,
But stedfast Rest of all things firmly stay'd
Upon the Pillours of Eternity,
That is contrair to *Mutability;*
For, all that moveth, doth in *Change* delight:
But thence-forth all shall rest eternally
With Him that is the God of Sabbaoth hight:
O that great Sabbaoth God, graunt me that Sabbaoth's sight.

115–116

Considering Mutability's presentation
of her case, and weighing her arguments,
I must admit that though not fitted for the role
of Heaven's Chief Executive, most certainly,
she had a case: I'm sick to death of seeing
this dodgy state of things, and alienated too
from all attachments in this so unperfect world,
those sky-flowers falling furiously.

But then I think of Nature's summing up,
about that time when no more change shall be,
but a settled fastness of all things firmly fixed
on everlasting grounds, set hard to withstand
Mutability's blitz. All that moves commotion
loves, is indisputable truth, but from here on in
all will be set fast at rest, with Him, my Lord
of Hosts. Haste, Lord, to make me fast!

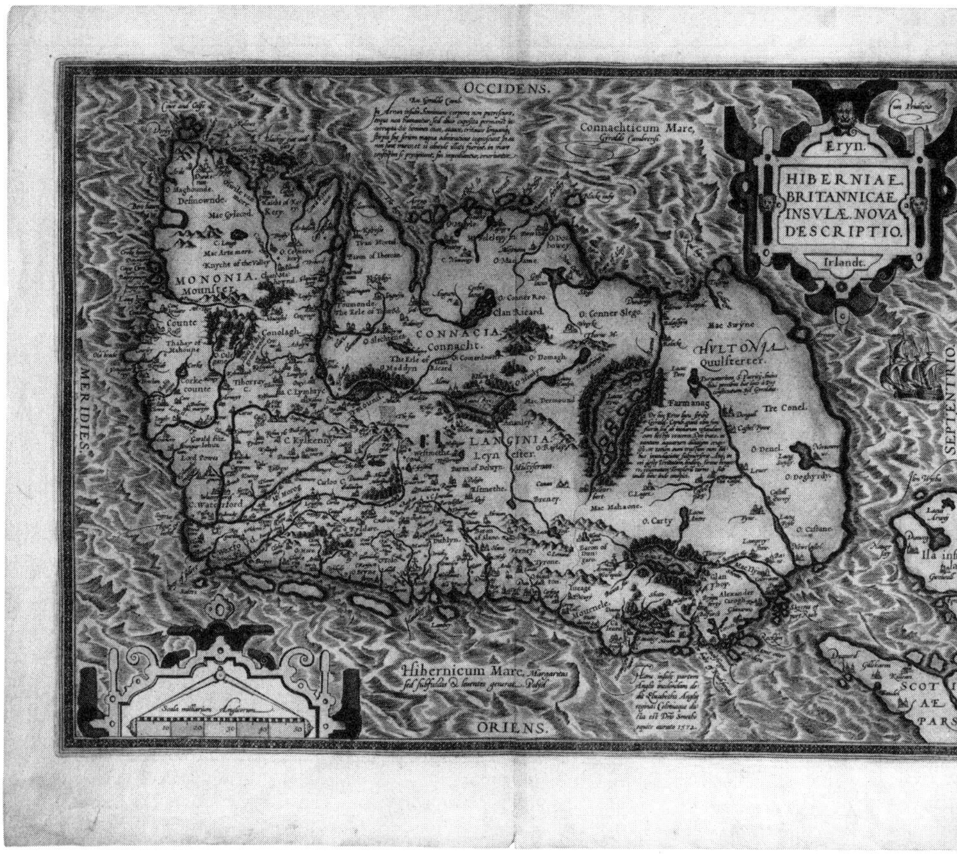
Eryn.
HIBERNIAE BRITANNICAE INSVLAE. NOVA DESCRIPTIO.
Irlandt.
OCCIDENS.
Connachticum Mare,
ORIENS.
Hibernicum Mare,
MERIDIES.
SEPTENTRIO.
MONONIA. Mounster.
CONNACIA. Connacht.
LANGINIA. Leynster.
HVLTONIA. Vlulsterter.
Desmownde.
Kery.
Clan Ricard.
Tre Conel.
Farmanag.
Mac Swyne
Mac Mahaone.
O. Carty
Tiberray
C. Kylkenny
Waterford
Dublyn
Breney
Conolagh
SCOTIAE PARS

ACKNOWLEDGEMENTS

As this book has been both long and short in the making, it must acknowledge two sorts of support, not always distinct. After stuttering attempts over about the three previous years, the text of the poem itself was written almost entirely in a single burst, during the month of April 2016, with only fine-tuning thereafter. To sustain that, it was very necessary to me to have readers with whom to engage, who would help me resolve the emerging jangle of registers into some sort of clarity, and I'm very grateful to Anna Pollert, Owen Joyce-Coughlan, Fergal Gaynor, Peter Manson, David Lloyd, Sarah Hayden, and Alison Croggon for having helped attune both the verse and myself.

It was at that point that Keith Tuma surprised me by suggesting that Miami University Press might publish *Fastness*. To take up that welcome offer, it was necessary that I get further out of my depth by writing an introduction. The scattered facts I've tried to shape there into some semblance of an argument reach back through more than three decades, to when Patricia Coughlan and Anne Fogarty first interested me in Spenser in Ireland, and I simultaneously discovered for myself my family's involvement with his writings, his reputation, and his legacy, in the form of William Petty's *Down Survey*. For generous assistance in expunging my worst errors of historical fact, I sincerely thank Thomas Herron, who deserves no blame for any lingering faults. And finally, for help in understanding what I was trying to do in relation to the diction of the poem, I thank Tom Leonard, for sending me a copy of his valuable anthology, *Radical Renfrew*, from which I quote, and also for the lingering memory of his own poetry, which often saved me from the "literary."

A NOTE FROM MIAMI UNIVERSITY PRESS ON THE TEXT

Trevor Joyce worked with the online text of Spenser's Mutabilitie Cantos available at David H. Radcliffe's archive *Spenser and the Tradition: English Poetry, 1579–1830: A Gathering of Texts, Biography, and Criticism*, which can be found at spenserians.cath .vt.edu/index.php. Professor Radcliffe indicates that the text of Spenser's poetry there

---

FACING: *Eryn. / HIBERNIAE, / BRITANNICAE / INSVLÆ, NOVA / DESCRIPTIO. / Irlandt.* (1592) by Abraham Ortelius (1527–1598), DCA00102. Dublin Castle Archival Material Collection.

is based on that of the 1715 Hughes edition of *The Faerie Queene* as scanned more than 20 years ago. At his recommendation we have consulted the Hughes edition and accordingly made a few small adjustments by way of modernizing spellings and so forth.

Thanks to David Radcliffe, James Bromley, and Kaara Peterson for their advice and interest in this project, to Jim Bricker and William M. Modrow of the Walter Havighurst Special Collections & Archives at Miami University's King Library for providing a scan of the Hughes edition, and to Alison Block and Amy Toland for their work with the Spenser text. Given the nature of this project we have preserved British/Irish spellings in Joyce's introduction and poem.

For fifty years, since publication of his first book in 1967, Trevor Joyce has been a unique voice in Irish writing. His books include *with the first dream of fire they hunt the cold* (New Writers' Press, 2001), *Courts of Airs and Earth* (Shearsman Books, 2006), *What's in Store* (New Writers' Press & The Gig, 2007), and *Selected Poems 1967–2014* (Shearsman Books, 2014). *Rome's Wreck* (Cusp Books, 2014) is a translation under constraint from the English of Edmund Spenser's *Ruines of Rome*.

His early work explored possibilities of the lyric, and began a lifelong engagement with translation. In the mid-seventies he gave up publishing and turned instead to the study of Chinese poetry, while working as a systems analyst in industry. His later work, following twenty years silence, is unparalleled within Irish poetry. Successive books explore the possibilities of found text, computer-mediated composition, writing under constraint, and radical approaches to translation.

Joyce co-founded, in Dublin, the New Writers' Press and its journal *The Lace Curtain* in the late sixties, and then the annual SoundEye Festival in Cork in the nineties. He has been included in representative anthologies, including the *Penguin Book of Irish Poetry* and the Oxford University Press *Anthology of Twentieth-Century British and Irish Poetry*. He was a Fulbright Scholar in 2002/3 and served as Visiting Fellow in Poetry to the University of Cambridge in 2009/10. He was elected to Aosdána, the Irish affiliation of artists, in 2004, and has been awarded in Italy the 2016 N.C. Kaser Poetry Prize.